This book belongs to:

Name

_____

_____

School

_____

_____

WELCOME TO 4th GRADE!

WORDS YOU SHOULD KNOW

Master these words fully before trying to move on. There are extra blank spelling test sheets at the back of the book for testing.

Spell each of your words by looking carefully at the spelling, covering the word up and then trying to write it by yourself.

ACT	ADDITION	AGE	AMERICA	APART	APPLE	APPLY
ARMS	BADLY	BALL	BANK	BATH	BEARABLE	BELT
BIGGEST	BILL	BLANK	BOLT	BONES	BOXES	BRAVE
BREATH	BRIGHTES	BRING	BRUSHES	BUILT	BUSHES	CARE
CAREFUL	CASE	CENTS	CHART	CHECK	CHEWABLE	CIRCLE
CLING	CLOTH	COIN	COLT	COMPASS	CONTEXT	COUCHES
COUGH	COWS	CRAFT	DAILY	DARKNESS	DASH	

Name _____

Date _____

WORDS YOU SHOULD KNOW

Master these words fully before trying to move on. There are extra blank spelling test sheets at the back of the book for testing.

Spell each of your words by looking carefully at the spelling, covering the word up and then trying to write it by yourself.

DEATH	DISH	DISHES	DIVISION	DOCK	DOLLARS	DOUGH

DRANK	DREAMER	DRIFT	DRINK	DRYER	EARS	ECHO

EDGE	EDUCATION	ENOUGH	EQUAL	FACE	FAIR	FASTEST

FEAR	FEATHER	FELT	FICTION	FIG	FIND	FLUTTER

FLYER	FORCE	FORGETFUL	FORM	FOXES	FREEDOM	FUNNEL

FUNNIEST	GIFT	GLADLY	GLASS	GONE	GOODNESS	GRAPH

Name _____

Date _____

WORDS YOU SHOULD KNOW

Master these words fully before trying to move on. There are extra blank spelling test sheets at the back of the book for testing.

Spell each of your words by looking carefully at the spelling, covering the word up and then trying to write it by yourself.

GROUP	GUIDE	HAPPINESS	HELPFUL	HELPFULNESS	HILL	HIMSELF

HOLIDAY	HONK	HOPEFUL	HOUR	HUSH	JOLT	JOYFUL

KEY	KINDNESS	KING	KNEW	LAUGH	LAVA	LAY

LEAD	LEARN	LEFT	LETTER	LIFT	LIKABLE	LIKENESS

LOCATION	LOCK	LOFT	LOUDEST	LOUDLY	LOVABLE	MADLY

MAGNET	MARCH	MATH	MEET	MELT	MESSES	METHOD

WORDS YOU SHOULD KNOW

Master these words fully before trying to move on. There are extra blank spelling test sheets at the back of the book for testing.

Spell each of your words by looking carefully at the spelling, covering the word up and then trying to write it by yourself.

MILE	MINUTE	MODEL	MONEY	MONTHS	MOTH	MOTHER

MOUTH	MUCH	NECK	OBSERVE	OUTCOME	PACK	PAINFUL

PAINTER	PARAGRAPH	PATCH	PATH	PENTAGON	PICTURE	PLANE

POWER	PREDICTION	PREFIX	PROBLEM	PROUDLY	QUACK	QUESTION

QUICK	QUICKLY	RAFT	RECTANGLE	RICH	RIDE	RING

ROAD	ROOT	ROPE	ROTATE	ROUGH	ROW	RUSHES

WORDS YOU SHOULD KNOW

Master these words fully before trying to move on. There are extra blank spelling test sheets at the back of the book for testing.

Spell each of your words by looking carefully at the spelling, covering the word up and then trying to write it by yourself.

SADLY	SALT	SCALE	SEARCH	SEASONS	SECOND	SEEDS
SELECT	SHIFT	SHORTEST	SHOULD	SHRINK	SICKNESS	SIFT
SILLIEST	SIMPLE	SING	SINGER	SINK	SIX	SIZABLE
SLING	SLOTH	SLOWEST	SLUSH	SMARTEST	SNACK	SOFT
SOFTEST	SOFTLY	SOUND	SPEAKER	SPRING	SQUARE	STACK
STARCH	STILL	STILT	STING	STINK	STORE	STRING

WORDS YOU SHOULD KNOW

Master these words fully before trying to move on. There are extra blank spelling test sheets at the back of the book for testing.

Spell each of your words by looking carefully at the spelling, covering the word up and then trying to write it by yourself.

STUDY	SUBTRACTION	SUCH	SUFFIX	SUN	SWIFT	TALL
TEACHER	THANK	THANKFUL	THING	THINK	THINKER	THOUGH
THOUGHTFUL	TONE	TOOTH	TORNADO	TOUGH	TRIUMPH	USABLE
USEFUL	VACATION	VOLCANO	WALL	WASH	WASHER	WASHES
WEEKLY	WELT	WHALE	WHAT	WHEN	WHERE	WHICH
WHILE	WHIP	WHIRL	WHISTLE	WHITE	WHOLE	WHY

Unit 1 Unscramble

Name: _____

Date: _____

ACRYLIC	ABUSE	AFFECTION	ACROSS	ABSOLUTE	ADVANCE
ADVENTURE	ADAGE	ACTOR	ACADEMIC	ADOPTION	ACTRESS

1. LTAUOSBE   _ _ _ _ _ _ T E

2. SUBAE   _ _ _ _ E

3. CAAMCDEI   A _ _ _ _ M _ _

4. RASCOS   _ _ R O _ _

5. LRCIAYC   A _ _ _ L _ _

6. TRAOC   _ C _ _ _

7. SSRECTA   _ _ T R _ _ _

8. EAGAD   _ _ A _ _

9. ODIANPTO   _ _ _ P _ _ _ N

10. VDNEAAC   _ _ V _ N _ _

11. EVRANUDET   A _ _ _ _ _ _ R _

12. NECTFFAIO   _ _ _ _ _ _ I _ N

Write a definition for each word. Underline the spelling words.

_____

_____

_____

_____

_____

_____

_____

Unit 1 Wordsearch

Search the words from the given list below. Words can be across, down, diagonally and spread out.

X	P	E	A	C	A	D	E	M	I	C	E
A	H	E	W	E	A	C	T	R	E	S	S
D	A	D	O	P	T	I	O	N	O	X	O
V	A	F	F	E	C	T	I	O	N	A	A
A	A	T	A	C	R	Y	L	I	C	B	D
N	I	D	A	C	T	O	R	K	R	S	V
C	X	A	A	C	R	P	W	M	O	O	E
E	C	A	C	G	Q	J	E	F	J	L	N
I	E	B	B	R	E	D	S	X	X	U	T
Q	C	H	N	U	O	L	Q	D	H	T	U
B	M	K	O	M	S	S	V	B	G	E	R
M	W	W	T	Y	E	E	S	V	J	Z	E

ABSOLUTE	ABUSE	ACADEMIC	ACROSS
ACRYLIC	ACTOR	ACTRESS	ADAGE
ADOPTION	ADVANCE	ADVENTURE	AFFECTION

Unit 1 Spelling

Name: _____

Date: _____

Circle the correct spelling for each word.

	A	B	C	D
1.	ABiOLUTE	ABSOLUTE	ABaOLUTE	ABSOLUxE
2.	ABgSE	ABUSE	ABgSb	ABUSi
3.	ACAdEflC	ACADEMIC	ACAddMIC	ACADrMIC
4.	ACROS	ACROSS	ACRISS	ACROw
5.	ACRYLIC	ACRYLnC	ACRYLIu	ACRYLIo
6.	ACTOx	ACTrR	ACTsR	ACTOR
7.	ACTRESS	ACTRES	ACkRESS	ACIRES
8.	ADiGj	ADAGj	ADhGE	ADAGE
9.	ADOPTIOt	ADOfTIOt	ADOPTION	ADdPTION
10.	ADVANCE	ADVAjCE	ADVAwCE	ADVANqE
11.	ADVENTURE	ADViNTURE	ADVENTcRE	ADVaNTURE
12.	AFFECTION	AFECTION	AFFECTgON	AFECTIoN

Write seven sentences using as many words from your spelling list as you can. Underline the spelling words.

1. ....

2. ....

3. ....

4. ....

5. ....

6. ....

7. ....

With permission Use an old magazine, newspaper or junk mail and find as many of your words in this unit you can (or the letters that make up your word). Cut it out, use a glue stick and paste it on your paper here.

Spelling Test

Your Answers	Correct Spelling If Incorrect
1	1
2	2
3	3
4	4
5	5
6	6
7	7
8	8
9	9
10	10
11	11
12	12
13	13
14	14
15	15
16	16
17	17
18	18
19	19
20	20

Unit 2 Unscramble

Name: _____

Date: _____

| ALOOF | APPOINT | ANYONE | ANYTHING | ALARM | ALREADY |
| ALTHOUGH | ALLIGATOR | ANKLE | AGAINST | ANTONYM | ALONE |

1. ATAGSIN   A _ _ _ N _ _

2. MALRA   A _ _ _ _

3. GTLIAOALR   A _ _ _ _ _ T _ _

4. LENAO   _ _ O _ _

5. LOFAO   _ _ _ O _

6. REYDALA   A _ _ _ A _ _

7. LHOUHGTA   A _ _ _ _ _ _ H

8. NLAKE   A _ _ _ _

9. MNYATNO   _ _ _ _ N _ M

10. NAEOYN   _ _ _ _ N E

11. NAYITNGH   _ _ Y T _ _ _ _

12. PNTAIPO   _ _ P O _ _ _

Write a definition for each word. Underline the spelling words.

_____

_____

_____

_____

_____

_____

_____

Unit 2 Wordsearch

Search the words from the given list below. Words can be across, down, diagonally and spread out.

```
A   L   T   H   O   U   G   H   O   J   A   B
I   H   S   A   L   R   E   A   D   Y   N   H
H   A   L   L   I   G   A   T   O   R   Y   Q
E   E   A   G   A   I   N   S   T   A   T   Z
A   Y   F   C   V   N   N   E   Z   N   H   M
A   P   K   A   L   O   N   E   U   K   I   H
L   N   P   D   U   G   S   C   K   L   N   C
D   A   T   O   C   L   H   J   C   E   G   A
F   P   L   O   I   A   N   Y   O   N   E   L
Q   M   H   O   N   N   N   A   I   S   I   A
Z   P   R   U   O   Y   T   H   T   R   L   R
K   H   V   D   U   F   M   G   N   F   I   M
```

AGAINST	ALARM	ALLIGATOR	ALONE
ALOOF	ALREADY	ALTHOUGH	ANKLE
ANTONYM	ANYONE	ANYTHING	APPOINT

Unit 2 Spelling

Name: _____

Date: _____

Circle the correct spelling for each word.

	A	B	C	D
1.	AGAIpST	AGAINSd	AGAdNSd	AGAINST
2.	ALARM	ALxRe	ALxRM	ALARb
3.	ALIGATOm	ALIGATOR	ALLIhATOR	ALLIGATOR
4.	ALObE	ALONh	ALbbE	ALONE
5.	ALOF	ALOOo	ALOOF	ALOv
6.	ALpEADq	ALREADY	ALpEADY	ALREsDY
7.	ALTHOUGH	ALTHOUjH	ALTHOUGu	ALTHOUGo
8.	ANwLE	ANKLE	ANKLy	ANwwE
9.	ANTOaYM	ANTOpYM	ANTONYM	ANTvpYM
10.	ANjONE	ANbONE	ANhONE	ANYONE
11.	ANYTqlbG	ANYTHhNG	ANYTqlNG	ANYTHING
12.	APOINT	APPsINT	APyINT	APPOINT

Write seven sentences using as many words from your spelling list as you can. Underline the spelling words.

1. ....

2. ....

3. ....

4. ....

5. ....

6. ....

7. ....

With permission Use an old magazine, newspaper or junk mail and find as many of your words in this unit you can (or the letters that make up your word). Cut it out, use a glue stick and paste it on your paper here.

Spelling Test

Your Answers	Correct Spelling If Incorrect
1	1
2	2
3	3
4	4
5	5
6	6
7	7
8	8
9	9
10	10
11	11
12	12
13	13
14	14
15	15
16	16
17	17
18	18
19	19
20	20

Unit 3 Unscramble

Name: _____

Date: _____

Let's put your puzzle solving skills to the test. Try unscrambling the words using the words in the box.

AVERAGE	ARCHITECTURE	AUSTRALIA	ASTRONOMY	ASKEW	ARTISTIC
APRICOT	ARRAY	AXIS	ATTRACTION	ARITHMETIC	ASIA

1. OTARPIC   A _ _ I _ _ _

2. ETEITHUCACRR   _ _ _ H _ _ _ _ _ U _ E

3. TEMRTIHCIA   _ _ I T H _ _ _ _ _

4. RRAYA   _ _ _ A _

5. SCTRIAIT   A _ _ _ _ _ I _

6. ISAA   A _ _ _

7. WASEK   _ S _ _ _

8. TSMAYOONR   _ _ T _ _ N _ _ _

9. OTRAATTNIC   A _ _ R _ C _ _ _ _

10. USLAAITAR   _ _ _ _ R _ _ _ A

11. GRAAEEV   A _ E _ _ _ _

12. ASIX   _ X _ _

Write a definition for each word. Underline the spelling words.

_____

_____

_____

_____

Unit 3 Wordsearch

Search the words from the given list below. Words can be across, down, diagonally and spread out.

Y	D	E	P	G	A	M	A	A	A	G	A
S	J	O	A	T	R	V	R	P	T	A	U
L	P	V	V	S	C	A	I	R	T	S	S
W	N	A	E	B	H	R	T	I	R	T	T
J	M	X	R	T	I	T	H	C	A	R	R
I	T	I	A	O	T	I	M	O	C	O	A
A	B	S	G	Z	E	S	E	T	T	N	L
B	S	I	E	Y	C	T	T	Z	I	O	I
V	L	I	A	J	T	I	I	C	O	M	A
P	P	R	A	V	U	C	C	N	N	Y	H
C	R	J	O	R	R	A	S	K	E	W	H
A	B	M	G	H	E	Q	K	D	L	C	S

APRICOT	ARCHITECTURE	ARITHMETIC	ARRAY
ARTISTIC	ASIA	ASKEW	ASTRONOMY
ATTRACTION	AUSTRALIA	AVERAGE	AXIS

Unit 3 Spelling

Name: _____

Date: _____

Circle the correct spelling for each word.

	A	B	C	D
1.	APRICOT	APRICuT	APRImoT	APRIgOT
2.	ARCHITECTURE	ARCHITECTURc	ARCHIqECTURc	ARCHITECIURE
3.	ARITaMETIC	ARITHMETeC	ARITHMETIC	ARITHMETIC
4.	ARRAY	ARyAs	ARAY	ARAi
5.	ARTeSTIC	ARTaSTIC	ARTISTIC	ARsISTIC
6.	ASqt	ASIA	ASqA	ASzA
7.	ASKEb	ASKqp	ASKEW	ASKqW
8.	ASTpONOMY	ASTRONdMY	ASTRONdyY	ASTRONOMY
9.	ATRACTbON	ATTRACTIOf	ATTRACTION	ATRACTION
10.	AUSTRALIa	AUSTRALIA	AUSTRALrA	AUSTRALIi
11.	AVERbvE	AVERAGE	AVERAvE	AVEwAGE
12.	AXIf	AXtv	AXIv	AXIS

Write seven sentences using as many words from your spelling list as you can. Underline the spelling words.

1. ....

2. ....

3. ....

4. ....

5. ....

6. ....

7. ....

With permission Use an old magazine, newspaper or junk mail and find as many of your words in this unit you can (or the letters that make up your word). Cut it out, use a glue stick and paste it on your paper here.

Spelling Test

Your Answers	Correct Spelling If Incorrect
1	1
2	2
3	3
4	4
5	5
6	6
7	7
8	8
9	9
10	10
11	11
12	12
13	13
14	14
15	15
16	16
17	17
18	18
19	19
20	20

Unit 4 Unscramble

Name: _____

Date: _____

Let's put your puzzle solving skills to the test. Try unscrambling the words using the words in the box.

BECAME	BANANA	BALLOT	BACKPACK	BALANCE	BARBER
BASIN	BANDIT	BARGAIN	BANQUET	BANDAGE	BARREL

1. CPKABACK   B _ _ _ _ _ _ K

2. ABANLEC   _ _ L _ _ C _

3. ABLLOT   _ _ L _ O _

4. NNAABA   _ _ N _ _ A

5. EDBGNAA   B A _ _ _ _ _

6. BITAND   _ A N _ _ _

7. EAQUTBN   _ _ _ Q _ E _

8. RBABER   _ _ _ B E _

9. ARBNGAI   _ _ _ G A _ _

10. REALRB   _ A _ _ _ L

11. BANSI   _ _ _ I _

12. CEEBMA   _ E C _ _ _

Write a definition for each word. Underline the spelling words.

_____

_____

_____

_____

_____

_____

Unit 4 Wordsearch

Search the words from the given list below. Words can be across, down, diagonally and spread out.

B	F	U	R	O	R	E	N	J	N	W	B
A	U	M	S	X	G	I	B	V	E	A	A
N	U	H	A	A	A	R	A	M	U	U	C
D	F	R	D	G	B	S	N	H	E	A	K
I	W	N	R	F	E	O	Q	S	E	M	P
T	A	A	B	B	C	F	U	N	Q	F	A
B	B	G	A	A	A	M	E	W	V	T	C
U	Z	P	R	L	M	U	T	J	V	Z	K
Q	G	W	R	L	E	B	A	R	B	E	R
D	B	W	E	O	B	A	N	A	N	A	E
G	L	E	L	T	Y	W	B	A	S	I	N
Q	E	B	A	L	A	N	C	E	G	A	V

BACKPACK	BALANCE	BALLOT	BANANA
BANDAGE	BANDIT	BANQUET	BARBER
BARGAIN	BARREL	BASIN	BECAME

Unit 4 Spelling

Circle the correct spelling for each word.

	A	B	C	D
1.	backpak	backpack	bakpack	bakpak
2.	ballance	ballence	balance	balence
3.	balut	balot	ballot	ballut
4.	banana	binana	banaa	binaa
5.	bandae	bandadge	bandea	bandage
6.	bandat	bandatt	banditt	bandit
7.	banquett	banqoet	banqoett	banquet
8.	birrber	barrber	birber	barber
9.	barrgian	bargian	bargain	barrgain
10.	barrel	birrel	birel	barel
11.	bascin	bassin	basin	basat
12.	becea	becime	became	becae

Write seven sentences using as many words from your spelling list as you can. Underline the spelling words.

1. _____

2. _____

3. _____

4. _____

5. _____

6. _____

7. _____

With permission Use an old magazine, newspaper or junk mail and find as many of your words in this unit you can (or the letters that make up your word). Cut it out, use a glue stick and paste it on your paper here.

Spelling Test

Your Answers	Correct Spelling If Incorrect
1	1
2	2
3	3
4	4
5	5
6	6
7	7
8	8
9	9
10	10
11	11
12	12
13	13
14	14
15	15
16	16
17	17
18	18
19	19
20	20

Unit 5 Unscramble

Let's put your puzzle solving skills to the test. Try unscrambling the words using the words in the box.

Believe	Blanket	Boast	Bother	Blown	Bleacher
Bracket	Bitter	Berry	Brass	Become	Breeze

1. OEEBCM   _ _ _ _ m e

7. WOBNL   _ _ _ w _

2. VIBLEEE   _ e _ i _ _ _

8. ASBTO   _ _ _ _ t

3. ERYBR   _ _ _ _ y

9. TRHBEO   _ o _ _ e _

4. ITBERT   _ _ t _ _ r

10. CTAERBK   _ _ _ _ k e _

5. KTBLNEA   _ _ a n _ _ _

11. BASSR   _ _ _ _ s

6. LECAHRBE   _ _ _ a _ _ e _

12. EREZBE   _ r e _ _ _

Write a definition for each word. Underline the spelling words.

_____

_____

_____

_____

_____

_____

_____

Unit 5

Search the words from the given list below. Words can be across, down, diagonally and spread out.

D	N	T	E	K	N	A	L	B	Y	M	D
N	L	I	V	Z	T	W	X	R	Y	Z	I
Z	D	V	E	L	B	N	Y	A	E	X	I
V	D	Q	I	Q	R	G	T	S	M	J	L
N	W	O	L	B	A	R	B	S	M	H	R
L	B	L	E	A	C	H	E	R	O	E	E
Q	T	R	B	E	K	P	C	H	Y	Q	T
G	D	S	E	T	E	F	O	L	T	B	T
L	O	K	A	E	T	L	M	W	S	O	I
F	H	O	G	O	Z	Y	E	D	N	F	B
N	H	I	Z	U	B	E	R	R	Y	A	K
Z	W	U	E	B	U	L	B	R	X	W	O

Become	Believe	Berry	Bitter
Blanket	Bleacher	Blown	Boast
Bother	Bracket	Brass	Breeze

With permission Use an old magazine, newspaper or junk mail and find as many of your words in this unit you can (or the letters that make up your word). Cut it out, use a glue stick and paste it on your paper here.

Spelling Test

Your Answers		Correct Spelling If Incorrect	
1		1	
2		2	
3		3	
4		4	
5		5	
6		6	
7		7	
8		8	
9		9	
10		10	
11		11	
12		12	
13		13	
14		14	
15		15	
16		16	
17		17	
18		18	
19		19	
20		20	

Unit 6 Unscramble

Let's put your puzzle solving skills to the test. Try unscrambling the words using the words in the box.

Bucket	Button	Bridal	Bridge	Bugle	Browser
Bubble	Bureau	Building	Broken	Brought	Brotherhood

1. RDIBAL   B _ _ d _ _

2. DIBGRE   _ _ _ _ g e

3. KBRNEO   _ _ _ k _ n

4. HRDOBERTHOO   _ r _ _ h _ _ _ o _ _

5. OTBHURG   _ _ o _ g _ _

6. BORWSRE   _ _ o _ s _ _

7. LUBBEB   _ u _ _ _ e

8. KEUTBC   _ u _ k _ _

9. LBEUG   _ _ _ _ e

10. LDUIIBGN   _ _ _ l _ i _ _

11. EBAURU   _ _ r _ _ u

12. NUBOTT   _ _ _ t o _

Write a definition for each word. Underline the spelling words.

_____

_____

_____

_____

_____

_____

Unit 6 Wordsearch

Search the words from the given list below. Words can be across, down, diagonally and spread out.

```
Y  H  N  B  T  G  H  F  P  N  I  G
C  I  B  C  A  E  T  L  L  M  M  N
M  X  G  L  B  U  T  T  O  N  S  I
I  A  B  U  B  B  L  E  R  S  W  D
W  R  I  T  R  Z  G  E  K  D  F  L
B  L  U  O  H  D  S  T  R  C  C  I
F  N  K  W  I  W  Q  Y  M  F  U  U
M  E  H  R  O  B  U  A  E  R  U  B
N  P  B  R  O  U  G  H  T  E  O  F
V  G  B  M  S  G  L  P  U  R  D  D
M  X  S  H  L  L  A  D  I  R  B  Y
B  R  O  T  H  E  R  H  O  O  D  D
```

Bridal	Bridge	Broken	Brotherhood
Brought	Browser	Bubble	Bucket
Bugle	Building	Bureau	Button

Unit 6 Spelling

Circle the correct spelling for each word.

	A	B	C	D
1.	Brradal	Bridal	Brridal	Bradal
2.	Brridje	Bridge	Bridje	Brridge
3.	Brroken	Brocken	Brrocken	Broken
4.	Brutherhod	Brotherhood	Brotherhoud	Brotherhod
5.	Brrooght	Brought	Brooght	Brrought
6.	Browcer	Brrowcer	Brrowser	Browser
7.	Buble	Boble	Bubble	Bobbwe
8.	Buket	Bucket	Buckett	Bukett
9.	Boglle	Bugle	Buglle	Bogze
10.	Boilding	Boillding	Buillding	Building
11.	Burreau	Buraeu	Burraeu	Bureau
12.	Boton	Button	Buton	Botton

Write seven sentences using as many words from your spelling list as you can. Underline the spelling words.

1. ....

2. ....

3. ....

4. ....

5. ....

6. ....

7. ....

With permission Use an old magazine, newspaper or junk mail and find as many of your words in this unit you can (or the letters that make up your word). Cut it out, use a glue stick and paste it on your paper here.

Spelling Test

Your Answers	Correct Spelling If Incorrect
1	1
2	2
3	3
4	4
5	5
6	6
7	7
8	8
9	9
10	10
11	11
12	12
13	13
14	14
15	15
16	16
17	17
18	18
19	19
20	20

Unit 7 Unscramble

Name: _____

Date: _____

Let's put your puzzle solving skills to the test. Try unscrambling the words using the words in the box.

Cannon	Cabbage	Calf	Canvas	Camouflage	Bytes
Canyon	Calm	Capture	Cable	Camera	Calendar

1. ESTBY   _ y _ _ _

2. BAECAGB   C _ b _ _ _ _

3. CEBLA   _ _ _ l _

4. ANREDCAL   _ _ _ e _ _ _ r

5. ALCF   _ _ _ f

6. LCAM   _ a _ _

7. ARAEMC   C a _ _ _ _

8. AUGAOMFLCE   C _ m _ _ _ _ _ g _

9. NONNAC   _ _ n _ o _

10. VCAASN   _ _ _ v a _

11. CAONNY   _ _ _ y _ n

12. APUECRT   _ _ _ t _ r _

Write a definition for each word. Underline the spelling words.

....

....

....

....

....

....

Unit 7 Wordsearch

Name: _____

Date: _____

Search the words from the given list below. Words can be across, down, diagonally and spread out.

C	A	J	A	K	G	V	S	C	T	B	H
G	I	T	L	P	V	A	M	J	C	B	S
V	X	O	X	R	N	L	R	K	C	D	A
E	I	Y	E	E	A	R	W	E	V	K	V
B	R	N	O	C	I	D	G	L	M	L	N
O	Z	O	K	K	Y	A	N	C	F	A	A
O	E	Y	Z	E	B	Y	T	E	S	F	C
W	Q	N	L	B	L	D	F	U	L	L	S
E	A	A	A	G	T	N	O	N	N	A	C
B	V	C	A	B	L	E	L	Z	C	C	C
I	B	H	C	Y	C	A	P	T	U	R	E
J	E	G	A	L	F	U	O	M	A	C	J

Bytes   Cabbage   Cable   Calendar

Calf   Calm   Camera   Camouflage

Cannon   Canvas   Canyon   Capture

Unit 7 Spelling

Circle the correct spelling for each word.

	A	B	C	D
1.	Bytes	Bytas	Byttas	Byttes
2.	Cabbadge	Cabbage	Cabage	Cabadge
3.	Cible	Ciblle	Cable	Cablle
4.	Cilendar	Callendar	Calendar	Cillendar
5.	Callph	Calph	Calf	Callf
6.	Callm	Calm	Cillm	Cilm
7.	Cimera	Camera	Cimerra	Camerra
8.	Camoufflage	Camouflage	Camooflage	Camoofflage
9.	Canrn	Cannon	Canun	Cannun
10.	Canvas	Cinvas	Cfnvass	Canvasc
11.	Canyon	Canyn	Canyun	Cinyn
12.	Capture	Captture	Captore	Capttore

Write seven sentences using as many words from your spelling list as you can. Underline the spelling words.

1. ....

2. ....

3. ....

4. ....

5. ....

6. ....

7. ....

With permission Use an old magazine, newspaper or junk mail and find as many of your words in this unit you can (or the letters that make up your word). Cut it out, use a glue stick and paste it on your paper here.

Spelling Test

Your Answers	Correct Spelling If Incorrect
1	1
2	2
3	3
4	4
5	5
6	6
7	7
8	8
9	9
10	10
11	11
12	12
13	13
14	14
15	15
16	16
17	17
18	18
19	19
20	20

Unit 8 Unscramble

Let's put your puzzle solving skills to the test. Try unscrambling the words using the words in the box.

Cartridge	Carrot	Cello	Carriage	Cattle	Carve
Carbon	Catch	Catcher	Carton	Caution	Celebrate
Castle					

1. ANCBOR   _ _ _ _ o n

2. CAGARREI   _ _ _ _ _ a _ e

3. RACTOR   C _ r _ _ _

4. TOCNAR   C _ _ t _ _

5. GRECAIRTD   _ _ r _ _ _ _ _ e

6. RAVCE   _ a _ _ _

7. ATSELC   _ a _ t _ _

8. CCTHA   _ _ t _ _

9. RCCTAEH   _ _ _ c _ e _

10. AETTLC   _ a _ _ _ e

11. UCANTIO   _ _ _ t _ o _

12. EEEBATRCL   C _ l _ _ _ _ _ _

13. LCOEL   _ _ l _ _

Write a definition for each word. Underline the spelling words.

....

....

....

....

....

Unit 8 Wordsearch

Search the words from the given list below. Words can be across, down, diagonally and spread out.

Z	F	H	C	A	R	T	R	I	D	G	E
T	N	C	A	T	C	H	E	R	N	H	E
I	P	T	A	L	Y	M	E	O	G	H	X
J	P	A	I	R	X	V	T	N	S	L	C
Q	R	C	T	I	R	R	O	L	L	E	C
F	O	H	C	W	A	I	Y	P	L	L	A
M	D	B	W	C	T	E	A	E	T	T	R
I	Z	T	N	U	A	V	B	G	W	S	R
D	Q	F	A	Q	P	R	V	D	E	A	O
O	A	C	E	P	A	A	B	G	S	C	T
E	O	G	S	T	G	C	R	O	N	X	W
T	E	N	E	L	T	T	A	C	N	U	O

Carbon	Carriage	Carrot	Carton	Cartridge
Carve	Castle	Catch	Catcher	Cattle
Caution	Celebrate	Cello		

Unit 8 Spelling

Circle the correct spelling for each word.

	A	B	C	D
1.	Carbon	Carbun	Carrbon	Carrbun
2.	Carraige	Caraige	Carriage	Cariage
3.	Carot	Carrut	Carut	Carrot
4.	Cartun	Carrtun	Carrton	Carton
5.	Cartridje	Cartridge	Carrtridge	Carrtridje
6.	Carve	Cirve	Carrve	Cirrve
7.	Castle	Cistle	Casctle	Casstle
8.	Citch	Catch	Cattch	Cittch
9.	Citcher	Cittcher	Cattcher	Catcher
10.	Catle	Cattle	Citle	Cittle
11.	Cauttion	Caution	Cautoin	Cauttoin
12.	Cellebrite	Cellebrate	Celebrate	Celebrite
13.	Celu	Cello	Celo	Cellu

Write seven sentences using as many words from your spelling list as you can. Underline the spelling words.

1. ....

2. ....

3. ....

4. ....

5. ....

6. ....

With permission Use an old magazine, newspaper or junk mail and find as many of your words in this unit you can (or the letters that make up your word). Cut it out, use a glue stick and paste it on your paper here.

Spelling Test

Your Answers	Correct Spelling If Incorrect
1	1
2	2
3	3
4	4
5	5
6	6
7	7
8	8
9	9
10	10
11	11
12	12
13	13
14	14
15	15
16	16
17	17
18	18
19	19
20	20

Unit 9 Unscramble

Let's put your puzzle solving skills to the test. Try unscrambling the words using the words in the box.

Chicken	Charge	Cirque	Chord	Century	Channel
Choir	Chapel	Character	Chain	Cherub	Certain
Charcoal	Centimeter				

1. TNMEERECIT   _ e _ t _ _ _ _ e _

2. YNETCRU   C _ _ _ _ _ y

3. IETRCAN   _ _ _ _ a i _

4. HANCI   C _ _ _ _

5. NAENLHC   C _ _ _ _ _ l

6. ECPLAH   _ h _ _ _ l

7. ACHRATREC   _ _ _ r _ c _ _ _

8. HLOACRAC   _ _ _ _ _ o a _

9. GHERCA   _ h _ r _ _

10. CHUERB   C h _ _ _ _

11. IHCKECN   _ _ i _ _ e _

12. CHROI   _ _ _ _ r

13. DCOHR   _ _ _ _ d

14. IQCERU   C _ _ q _ _

Write a definition for each word. Underline the spelling words.

....

....

....

....

....

Unit 9 Wordsearch

Search the words from the given list below. Words can be across, down, diagonally and spread out.

Y	F	O	O	B	B	U	R	E	H	C	L
P	M	L	M	I	T	W	R	Y	L	H	A
R	G	O	Z	L	C	I	B	V	Q	A	O
E	C	N	C	G	O	H	U	L	G	P	C
T	C	E	C	H	A	R	A	C	T	E	R
E	G	K	C	C	A	V	Q	N	I	L	A
M	X	C	V	E	E	I	B	K	N	M	H
I	E	I	Y	R	U	T	N	E	C	E	C
T	G	H	K	T	J	P	O	Z	H	F	L
N	C	C	H	A	R	G	E	I	O	F	V
E	U	Q	R	I	C	R	G	X	R	T	B
C	Y	T	F	N	C	X	T	E	D	A	W

Centimeter	Century	Certain	Chain	Channel
Chapel	Character	Charcoal	Charge	Cherub
Chicken	Choir	Chord	Cirque	

Unit 9 Spelling

Circle the correct spelling for each word.

	A	B	C	D
1.	Centtameter	Centameter	Centtimeter	Centimeter
2.	Centtory	Centory	Centtury	Century
3.	Cerrtain	Certian	Cerrtian	Certain
4.	Chdi	Chian	Chaan	Chain
5.	Chinel	Chanel	Channel	Chinnel
6.	Chapell	Chipell	Chipel	Chapel
7.	Character	Chirracter	Chiracter	Charracter
8.	Charrcual	Charcual	Charcoal	Charrcoal
9.	Charje	Charrje	Charrge	Charge
10.	Cherub	Cherob	Cherrob	Cherrub
11.	Chicken	Chiken	Chickn	Chikn
12.	Chiorr	Choir	Chior	Choirr
13.	Churrd	Churd	Chorrd	Chord
14.	Cirque	Cirrqoe	Cirqoe	Cirrque

Write seven sentences using as many words from your spelling list as you can. Underline the spelling words.

1. ....

2. ....

3. ....

4. ....

5. ....

6. ....

With permission Use an old magazine, newspaper or junk mail and find as many of your words in this unit you can (or the letters that make up your word). Cut it out, use a glue stick and paste it on your paper here.

Spelling Test

Your Answers	Correct Spelling If Incorrect
1	1
2	2
3	3
4	4
5	5
6	6
7	7
8	8
9	9
10	10
11	11
12	12
13	13
14	14
15	15
16	16
17	17
18	18
19	19
20	20

Unit 10 Unscramble

Name: _____

Date: _____

Let's put your puzzle solving skills to the test. Try unscrambling the words using the words in the box.

Citizenship	Claim	Community	Coach	Closure	Compassion
Clause	College	Comedy	Compass	Coastal	Collection
Comment	Commute	Colon			

1. PIISTCZNHIE   _ _ _ _ _ e _ s _ _ p

2. MICLA   _ _ a _ _

3. EACSLU   _ _ _ u s _

4. LOURESC   C _ _ _ _ _ e

5. CHOCA   _ _ a _ _

6. ATLAOSC   _ o _ _ t _ _

7. NLOCLEIOCT   C _ _ _ _ c _ _ o _

8. EOGELCL   _ _ _ _ e g _

9. ONLOC   _ _ _ o _

10. YEOCMD   _ _ _ e d _

11. OTCNEMM   _ o _ _ e _ _

12. MCYUOTIMN   C _ m _ _ _ _ _ _

13. TUOMCEM   C _ _ _ _ t _

14. SSACPMO   C _ m _ _ _ _

15. SOSONCAIMP   C _ _ p _ _ _ _ o _

Write a definition for each word. Underline the spelling words.

....

....

....

....

....

Unit 10 Wordsearch

Search the words from the given list below. Words can be across, down, diagonally and spread out.

```
C  G  N  O  I  S  S  A  P  M  O  C
I  N  F  E  E  G  V  C  U  C  O  O
T  A  Q  C  O  L  O  N  E  L  C  M
I  D  H  C  A  L  G  S  L  O  O  E
Z  K  S  A  L  V  U  E  E  S  M  D
E  P  O  E  Z  A  C  C  T  U  M  Y
N  R  G  J  L  T  I  O  U  R  U  O
S  E  D  C  I  C  O  M  M  E  N  T
H  Q  W  O  O  O  L  P  M  O  I  O
I  F  N  A  B  H  V  A  O  P  T  X
P  F  C  O  Y  N  T  S  C  V  Y  O
V  H  O  P  L  A  T  S  A  O  C  V
```

Citizenship	Claim	Clause	Closure	Coach
Coastal	Collection	College	Colon	Comedy
Comment	Community	Commute	Compass	Compassion

Unit 10 Spelling

Name: _____

Date: _____

Circle the correct spelling for each word.

	A	B	C	D
1.	Citizenship	Cittizenship	Cattizenship	Catizenship
2.	Claim	Cliam	Cllaim	Clliam
3.	Cllause	Cluase	Clluase	Clause
4.	Cllousure	Closure	Cllosure	Clousure
5.	Cuach	Coah	Coach	Cuah
6.	Coastal	Cuastal	Coasctal	Coasstal
7.	Collectoin	Colection	Collection	Colectoin
8.	Colege	Colleje	Coleje	College
9.	Culon	Colon	Collon	Cullon
10.	Comedy	Cumedy	Comey	Comay
11.	Coment	Comment	Conment	Comnment
12.	Comunity	Comonity	Community	Commonity
13.	Comote	Commute	Commotp	Comute
14.	Cumpas	Compass	Compas	Compasc
15.	Compassoin	Compasoin	Compassion	Compasion

Write four sentences using as many words from your spelling list as you can. Underline the spelling words.

1. ....

2. ....

3. ....

4. ....

With permission Use an old magazine, newspaper or junk mail and find as many of your words in this unit you can (or the letters that make up your word). Cut it out, use a glue stick and paste it on your paper here.

Spelling Test

Your Answers	Correct Spelling If Incorrect
1	1
2	2
3	3
4	4
5	5
6	6
7	7
8	8
9	9
10	10
11	11
12	12
13	13
14	14
15	15
16	16
17	17
18	18
19	19
20	20

Unit 11 Unscramble

Name: _____

Date: _____

Let's put your puzzle solving skills to the test. Try unscrambling the words using the words in the box.

Compatible	Computer	Compose	Contact	Construction	Contain
Congress	Completion	Contest	Conductor	Complete	Conservation
Cookies	Continent				

1. EOLAPIMCBT   C _ _ p _ _ _ _ l _

2. TLEMEOPC   _ o _ p _ _ _ _

3. CEMNLOTIPO   _ o _ _ l _ _ i _ _

4. PSMEOOC   _ o _ _ _ s _

5. CRUMTEPO   _ _ _ _ u _ e _

6. TOUDONRCC   _ _ _ _ _ _ t _ r

7. CORSGNSE   _ _ _ _ r _ s _

8. RNOANOESTVIC   C _ _ s _ _ _ a _ _ _ _

9. UORCSNNOTTCI   _ _ n s t _ _ _ _ _ _ _

10. CATCTNO   C _ n _ _ _ _

11. TAOINCN   _ _ _ t _ i _

12. OTCENST   _ _ n _ _ _ t

13. NNONTICET   _ _ _ t _ n _ _ _

14. OSEOKCI   _ o _ k _ _ _

Write a definition for each word. Underline the spelling words.

....

....

Unit 11 Wordsearch

Search the words from the given list below. Words can be across, down, diagonally and spread out.

N	O	I	T	A	V	R	E	S	N	O	C
C	C	W	C	O	N	T	E	S	T	H	L
Y	O	U	O	T	C	A	T	N	O	C	C
E	M	N	N	C	O	M	G	C	M	O	O
S	P	C	T	R	O	G	R	E	Q	M	N
S	L	Y	I	A	K	M	R	R	F	P	D
E	E	W	N	R	I	L	P	Z	W	O	U
R	T	L	E	E	E	N	N	U	V	S	C
G	E	F	N	X	S	D	L	Y	T	E	T
N	O	I	T	E	L	P	M	O	C	E	O
O	E	L	B	I	T	A	P	M	O	C	R
C	O	N	S	T	R	U	C	T	I	O	N

Compatible	Complete	Completion	Compose	Computer
Conductor	Congress	Conservation	Construction	Contact
Contain	Contest	Continent	Cookies	

Unit 11 Spelling

Circle the correct spelling for each word.

	A	B	C	D
1.	Compattible	Compattable	Compatable	Compatible
2.	Complete	Cumplete	Compllete	Cumpllete
3.	Complletoin	Completion	Completoin	Complletion
4.	Compousse	Compose	Composse	Compouse
5.	Compotter	Compoter	Computter	Computer
6.	Condoctor	Condocttor	Conductor	Conducttor
7.	Congress	Cungres	Congresc	Congres
8.	Consservatoin	Consservation	Conservation	Conservatoin
9.	Constructoin	Consstruction	Consstructoin	Construction
10.	Conttact	Contact	Cunttact	Cuntact
11.	Contian	Conttain	Conttian	Contain
12.	Contest	Conttest	Cuntest	Cunttest
13.	Cunttinent	Continent	Cuntinent	Conttinent
14.	Cokies	Cookeis	Cokeis	Cookies

Write four sentences using as many words from your spelling list as you can. Underline the spelling words.

1. ....

2. ....

3. ....

4. ....

With permission Use an old magazine, newspaper or junk mail and find as many of your words in this unit you can (or the letters that make up your word). Cut it out, use a glue stick and paste it on your paper here.

Spelling Test

Your Answers

1
2
3
4
5
6
7
8
9
10
11
12
13
14
15
16
17
18
19
20

Correct Spelling If Incorrect

1
2
3
4
5
6
7
8
9
10
11
12
13
14
15
16
17
18
19
20

Unit 12 Unscramble

Name: _____

Date: _____

Let's put your puzzle solving skills to the test. Try unscrambling the words using the words in the box.

Council	Crocodile	Courage	Corona	Cotton	Couldn't
Crew	Course	Corruption	Corner	Creature	Covered
Credit	Copper				

1. PCRPEO   _ _ _ _ e r

2. CRRONE   C _ r _ _ _

3. CORANO   _ _ r _ a

4. ICPTOORUNR   _ o _ _ u _ _ _ n

5. NCTTOO   _ o _ _ n

6. TCLN'DUO   _ _ _ l _ _ _ t

7. CCUNLIO   _ _ u _ _ _ l

8. UCRGEAO   _ o _ _ _ g _

9. SUEORC   _ _ _ r s _

10. VERDOCE   C _ _ _ r _ _

11. RRAUETEC   _ r _ a _ _ _ _

12. IETCDR   C _ _ _ _ t

13. WRCE   C _ _ _

14. EODCLROCI   _ r _ _ o _ _ _ _

Write a definition for each word. Underline the spelling words.

_____

_____

_____

_____

_____

_____

Unit 12 Wordsearch

Name: _____

Date: _____

Search the words from the given list below. Words can be across, down, diagonally and spread out.

```
C   O   U   L   D   N   '   T   L   X   P   N
X   C   O   R   R   U   P   T   I   O   N   M
A   F   B   A   L   C   B   I   H   T   M   J
E   S   C   W   I   S   R   D   R   A   C   O
L   S   C   K   C   V   J   E   W   O   D   Y
I   W   R   E   N   U   N   R   W   Y   E   Z
D   K   E   U   U   R   R   C   C   A   R   W
O   G   A   N   O   T   T   O   C   N   E   X
C   K   T   C   C   C   P   T   Q   O   V   E
O   B   U   S   M   P   F   O   P   R   O   V
R   P   R   N   E   G   A   R   U   O   C   D
C   M   E   R   W   K   Y   W   Q   C   Y   R
```

Copper	Corner	Corona	Corruption	Cotton
Couldn't	Council	Courage	Course	Covered
Creature	Credit	Crew	Crocodile	

Unit 12 Spelling

Circle the correct spelling for each word.

	A	B	C	D
1.	Copper	Cuper	Copvr	Cunper
2.	Currner	Curner	Corrner	Corner
3.	Corona	Corrona	Curona	Currona
4.	Coruptoin	Corruptoin	Corruption	Coruption
5.	Cotton	Cuton	Coton	Cutton
6.	Coulldn't	Coolldn't	Cooldn't	Couldn't
7.	Cooncil	Cooncill	Council	Councill
8.	Courage	Coorrage	Coorage	Courrage
9.	Coorse	Coorrse	Courrse	Course
10.	Cuvered	Coverred	Cuverred	Covered
11.	Crreature	Crraeture	Craeture	Creature
12.	Crredat	Credat	Credit	Crredit
13.	Crew	Crraw	Cras	Crrew
14.	Crucodile	Crocodile	Crrocodile	Crrucodile

Write four sentences using as many words from your spelling list as you can. Underline the spelling words.

1. ....

2. ....

3. ....

4. ....

With permission Use an old magazine, newspaper or junk mail and find as many of your words in this unit you can (or the letters that make up your word). Cut it out, use a glue stick and paste it on your paper here.

Spelling Test

Your Answers	Correct Spelling If Incorrect
1	1
2	2
3	3
4	4
5	5
6	6
7	7
8	8
9	9
10	10
11	11
12	12
13	13
14	14
15	15
16	16
17	17
18	18
19	19
20	20

Unit 13 Unscramble

Let's put your puzzle solving skills to the test. Try unscrambling the words using the words in the box.

Debris	Crust	Decide	Dental	Customary	Decade
Crowd	Crumble	Crusher	Decode	Demand	Deceive
Damage	Crooked				

1. EKDCROO _ _ _ _ _ e d

2. RDWCO _ _ o _ _

3. MCLRUBE _ _ _ _ b _ e

4. USRHERC C _ _ _ h _ _

5. RCSUT _ _ u _ _

6. UCAMOTSRY C _ s _ _ _ _ _ _

7. DMAAEG _ _ m _ _ e

8. RBESDI _ _ _ _ i s

9. CEADDE _ _ _ _ d e

10. EIDEECV _ _ c _ _ v _

11. EDIECD _ _ c _ _ e

12. EDCDOE D _ _ o _ _

13. ADDEMN D _ _ a _ _

14. NDTALE D _ n _ _ _

Write a definition for each word. Underline the spelling words.

....

....

....

....

....

....

Unit 13 Wordsearch

Name: _____

Date: _____

Search the words from the given list below. Words can be across, down, diagonally and spread out.

B	O	Z	T	X	S	L	P	D	W	O	U
E	G	A	M	A	D	E	C	E	I	V	E
S	E	I	N	E	V	D	V	R	T	Q	E
I	B	P	C	C	E	D	E	S	E	C	Q
R	J	O	D	R	Y	D	J	M	D	H	M
B	D	A	E	U	U	X	I	H	A	D	Z
E	E	V	K	M	M	S	I	C	C	N	S
D	A	O	O	B	L	A	T	N	E	D	D
Z	Z	U	O	L	C	R	O	W	D	D	V
Y	X	U	R	E	H	S	U	R	C	A	C
T	O	S	C	U	S	T	O	M	A	R	Y
X	S	N	K	D	L	F	T	F	Z	A	D

Crooked	Crowd	Crumble	Crusher	Crust
Customary	Damage	Debris	Decade	Deceive
Decide	Decode	Demand	Dental	

Unit 13 Spelling

Circle the correct spelling for each word.

	A	B	C	D
1.	Crouked	Crockeo	Croked	Crooked
2.	Crrowd	Crowd	Crruwd	Cruwd
3.	Cromble	Crromble	Crumble	Crrumble
4.	Crrusher	Crosher	Crusher	Crrosher
5.	Crrust	Crrost	Crost	Crust
6.	Cusctomary	Customary	Cusstomary	Costomary
7.	Damadge	Damea	Damae	Damage
8.	Debrras	Debrris	Debras	Debris
9.	Decade	Deciqe	Decea	Decae
10.	Decieve	Deceive	Desieve	Deseive
11.	Decide	Decei	Decie	Decadl
12.	Decue	Decode	Decude	Decoe
13.	Demad	Demand	Demid	Demind
14.	Denttil	Denttal	Dental	Dencil

Write four sentences using as many words from your spelling list as you can. Underline the spelling words.

1. ....

2. ....

3. ....

4. ....

With permission Use an old magazine, newspaper or junk mail and find as many of your words in this unit you can (or the letters that make up your word). Cut it out, use a glue stick and paste it on your paper here.

Spelling Test

Your Answers	Correct Spelling If Incorrect
1	1
2	2
3	3
4	4
5	5
6	6
7	7
8	8
9	9
10	10
11	11
12	12
13	13
14	14
15	15
16	16
17	17
18	18
19	19
20	20

Unit 14 Unscramble

Name: _____

Date: _____

Let's put your puzzle solving skills to the test. Try unscrambling the words using the words in the box.

Determine	Develop	Digestion	Departure	Diet	Destroy
Deposit	Diamond	Depression	Dictionary	Digital	Devotion
Depend					

1. UEDPRATRE   _ _ _ _ _ t _ r _

2. PEDNED   D e _ _ _ _

3. ITPESDO   D _ _ _ _ _ t

4. SPNESRIDOE   D _ _ _ _ _ s i _ _

5. ESTRYDO   D _ _ _ r _ _

6. NEERTIDME   _ _ _ e _ _ _ n _

7. LEVPEOD   _ _ _ _ l _ p

8. DNVOOITE   _ _ v _ _ _ _ n

9. ADONDMI   _ _ _ m _ n _

10. CYAIRITDON   D _ _ t _ _ n _ _ _

11. TIED   _ i _ _

12. IODSGNETI   _ _ _ e _ t _ _ _

13. ALIDGIT   D _ _ _ t _ _

Write a definition for each word. Underline the spelling words.

....

....

....

....

....

Unit 14 Wordsearch

Name: _____

Date: _____

Search the words from the given list below. Words can be across, down, diagonally and spread out.

```
R   X   D   E   P   R   E   S   S   I   O   N
T   Y   R   A   N   O   I   T   C   I   D   I
W   E   R   U   T   R   A   P   E   D   Z   Z
L   N   I   C   P   F   D   E   P   E   N   D
E   I   T   D   E   S   T   R   O   Y   O   E
D   M   D   I   G   I   T   A   L   G   I   V
D   R   I   N   S   U   R   I   E   F   T   O
A   E   C   E   O   O   O   U   V   H   S   T
U   T   O   U   I   M   P   J   E   K   E   I
Q   E   A   O   D   P   A   E   D   G   G   O
Z   D   H   T   Z   D   J   I   D   F   I   N
K   I   R   V   K   R   P   B   D   N   D   J
```

Departure	Depend	Deposit	Depression	Destroy
Determine	Develop	Devotion	Diamond	Dictionary
Diet	Digestion	Digital		

Unit 14 Spelling

Circle the correct spelling for each word.

	A	B	C	D
1.	Deparrture	Deparrtore	Departore	Departure
2.	Dapend	Deped	Depend	Daped
3.	Depoussit	Depousit	Depossit	Deposit
4.	Depression	Depresion	Depresoin	Depressoin
5.	Desstroy	Destroy	Destruy	Desctroy
6.	Dettermane	Determine	Dettermine	Determane
7.	Develup	Develop	Devellop	Devellup
8.	Devottion	Devotoin	Devottoin	Devotion
9.	Daimond	Diamund	Diamond	Daimund
10.	Dictionary	Dicttoinary	Dicttionary	Dictoinary
11.	Deitt	Deit	Diett	Diet
12.	Digestoin	Digesstoin	Digestion	Digesstion
13.	Dagittal	Digital	Digittal	Dagital

Write four sentences using as many words from your spelling list as you can. Underline the spelling words.

1. ....

2. ....

3. ....

4. ....

With permission Use an old magazine, newspaper or junk mail and find as many of your words in this unit you can (or the letters that make up your word). Cut it out, use a glue stick and paste it on your paper here.

Spelling Test

Your Answers		Correct Spelling If Incorrect	
1		1	
2		2	
3		3	
4		4	
5		5	
6		6	
7		7	
8		8	
9		9	
10		10	
11		11	
12		12	
13		13	
14		14	
15		15	
16		16	
17		17	
18		18	
19		19	
20		20	

Unit 15 Unscramble

Name: _____

Date: _____

Let's put your puzzle solving skills to the test. Try unscrambling the words using the words in the box.

Dwelling	Disruption	Drill	Drama	Duet	During
Dimple	Dolphin	Discuss	District	Dragon	Dimension
Dispersal	Distraction				

1. NDONIIMES _ _ _ e n _ _ _ _

2. LMEDPI D _ m _ _ _

3. SUDCSSI _ i _ c _ _ _

4. SERLADPIS _ _ _ p _ _ s _ _

5. SDIPTONURI _ i _ _ _ p t _ _ _

6. IRDONSACTIT _ _ s _ _ _ c _ _ o _

7. TRDITCSI D _ _ t _ _ _ _

8. POLHIDN D o _ _ _ _ _

9. RAODNG D _ a _ _ _

10. AARDM _ _ _ _ a

11. LLIRD _ r _ _ _

12. EUTD D _ _ _

13. RNIGUD D _ _ _ n _

14. GWEILDLN _ _ _ l _ i _ _

Write a definition for each word. Underline the spelling words.

....

....

....

....

....

Unit 15 Wordsearch

Search the words from the given list below. Words can be across, down, diagonally and spread out.

Y	L	T	M	S	E	L	P	M	I	D	R
S	S	U	C	S	I	D	A	Y	G	A	N
L	U	G	N	I	L	L	E	W	D	O	O
A	Y	A	M	A	R	D	A	D	Z	U	I
S	Y	Z	J	D	A	T	R	U	Z	X	T
R	N	D	U	R	U	N	S	R	M	T	C
E	N	O	I	S	N	E	M	I	D	X	A
P	D	L	G	D	O	E	T	N	D	R	R
S	X	P	W	A	S	Y	N	G	N	Z	T
I	L	H	E	D	R	I	L	L	R	E	S
D	Y	I	N	M	I	D	D	R	I	B	I
Z	I	N	O	I	T	P	U	R	S	I	D

Dimension	Dimple	Discuss	Dispersal	Disruption
Distraction	District	Dolphin	Dragon	Drama
Drill	Duet	During	Dwelling	

Unit 15 Spelling

Name: _____

Date: _____

Circle the correct spelling for each word.

	A	B	C	D
1.	Dimensoin	Dimenssoin	Dimension	Dimenssion
2.	Damplle	Dimple	Dimplle	Dample
3.	Discuss	Dissuss	Disdus	Dissus
4.	Daspersal	Dispersal	Disspersal	Discpersal
5.	Disruptoin	Dissruption	Dissruptoin	Disruption
6.	Disstraction	Distractoin	Disstractoin	Distraction
7.	Disstrict	Dastrict	Disctrict	District
8.	Dolfin	Dollphin	Dolphin	Dollfin
9.	Dradgon	Drradgon	Drragon	Dragon
10.	Drama	Drrima	Drima	Drrama
11.	Dral	Drall	Dril	Drill
12.	Duett	Duet	Doett	Doet
13.	Doring	Dorring	During	Durring
14.	Dwelling	Dweling	Dwellang	Dwelang

Write four sentences using as many words from your spelling list as you can. Underline the spelling words.

1. ....

2. ....

3. ....

4. ....

With permission Use an old magazine, newspaper or junk mail and find as many of your words in this unit you can (or the letters that make up your word). Cut it out, use a glue stick and paste it on your paper here.

Spelling Test

Your Answers	Correct Spelling If Incorrect
1	1
2	2
3	3
4	4
5	5
6	6
7	7
8	8
9	9
10	10
11	11
12	12
13	13
14	14
15	15
16	16
17	17
18	18
19	19
20	20

Unit 16 Unscramble

Let's put your puzzle solving skills to the test. Try unscrambling the words using the words in the box.

Elevation	Electricity	Ecosystem	Elephant	Eighteen	Elected
Elbow	Eighty	Eclipse	Earthquake	Early	Ecology
Either					

1. RLAYE   E _ _ _ _

2. ERETKAUHAQ   E a _ _ h _ _ _ _ _

3. PEELCIS   _ c _ _ p _ _

4. OOCLEYG   _ _ o l _ _ _

5. YSCMOESTE   _ c _ _ _ s _ _ _

6. ETHEIEGN   E i _ _ _ _ _ _

7. HETYGI   _ i _ _ _ y

8. HTEIER   _ _ _ h _ r

9. WBLEO   _ _ _ o _

10. CTEEEDL   _ _ _ _ t _ d

11. ILCIREYETCT   E _ _ _ t _ i _ _ _ _

12. PENALTEH   _ l _ _ h _ _ _

13. TEEAVLNOI   E _ _ v _ _ _ _ _

Write a definition for each word. Underline the spelling words.

....

....

....

....

....

Unit 16 Wordsearch

Search the words from the given list below. Words can be across, down, diagonally and spread out.

R	O	O	M	K	X	Q	I	K	Q	W	A
I	E	Z	Q	E	S	V	I	R	P	E	T
O	A	E	S	L	D	Z	E	A	M	L	I
L	R	M	T	N	A	H	P	E	L	E	E
D	T	E	H	M	T	Q	T	W	I	C	I
L	H	S	B	I	E	S	U	G	N	T	G
V	Q	P	E	H	Y	A	H	D	W	E	H
W	U	I	X	S	E	T	R	N	F	D	T
J	A	L	O	F	E	C	O	L	O	G	Y
C	K	C	A	E	L	B	O	W	Y	M	N
J	E	E	N	O	I	T	A	V	E	L	E
K	Y	T	I	C	I	R	T	C	E	L	E

Early   Earthquake   Eclipse   Ecology   Ecosystem

Eighteen   Eighty   Either   Elbow   Elected

Electricity   Elephant   Elevation

Unit 16 Spelling

Circle the correct spelling for each word.

	A	B	C	D
1.	Eirly	Earrly	Eirrly	Early
2.	Earrthqauke	Earrthquake	Earthquake	Earthqauke
3.	Eclipse	Eclipce	Ecllipse	Ecllipce
4.	Eculogy	Ecollogy	Ecullogy	Ecology
5.	Ecousystem	Ecossystem	Ecoussystem	Ecosystem
6.	Eightean	Eighteen	Eaghten	Eighten
7.	Eighty	Eightty	Eaghty	Eaghtty
8.	Eather	Eatther	Either	Eitther
9.	Ellbow	Ellbuw	Elbow	Elbuw
10.	Elected	Elacted	Ellacted	Ellected
11.	Electricity	Ellectracity	Ellectricity	Electracity
12.	Elephant	Elefant	Ellephant	Ellefant
13.	Ellevation	Elevation	Elevatoin	Ellevatoin

Write four sentences using as many words from your spelling list as you can. Underline the spelling words.

1. ....

2. ....

3. ....

4. ....

With permission Use an old magazine, newspaper or junk mail and find as many of your words in this unit you can (or the letters that make up your word). Cut it out, use a glue stick and paste it on your paper here.

Spelling Test

Your Answers	Correct Spelling If Incorrect
1	1
2	2
3	3
4	4
5	5
6	6
7	7
8	8
9	9
10	10
11	11
12	12
13	13
14	14
15	15
16	16
17	17
18	18
19	19
20	20

Unit 17 Unscramble

Name: _____

Date: _____

Let's put your puzzle solving skills to the test. Try unscrambling the words using the words in the box.

Europe	Envelope	Energy	English	Engineer	Emotion
Emerald	Erratic	Equation	Eleven	Elevator	Equator
Erosion					

1. TERAOLVE   _ _ e _ a _ _ _

2. ELEVNE   _ _ e _ _ n

3. DRLMAEE   _ m e _ _ _ _

4. ETIMONO   _ _ o t _ _ _

5. ENGYER   _ _ e _ g _

6. NERGEEIN   _ _ _ i _ e _ _

7. GSHINLE   _ _ _ l _ s _

8. OEEPLNVE   _ _ _ _ l _ _ e

9. INUATQEO   _ _ _ a _ _ o _

10. UEAQROT   _ _ u a _ _ _

11. SERINOO   _ _ _ s _ _ n

12. ARTCERI   _ _ _ _ _ i c

13. EERPOU   _ u _ _ _ e

Write a definition for each word. Underline the spelling words.

Unit 17 Wordsearch

Search the words from the given list below. Words can be across, down, diagonally and spread out.

Q	O	V	S	K	T	K	F	P	H	R	J
Z	R	O	T	A	U	Q	E	H	H	L	A
Y	T	B	J	H	S	I	L	G	N	E	E
Q	E	E	D	K	W	Y	L	O	B	U	N
N	N	M	J	N	G	P	I	Y	F	S	V
O	G	H	E	R	O	T	A	V	E	L	E
I	I	J	E	R	A	I	C	E	T	E	L
S	N	N	A	U	A	E	T	P	J	L	O
O	E	L	Q	U	P	L	N	O	A	E	P
R	E	E	Q	O	F	C	D	R	M	V	E
E	R	R	A	T	I	C	L	U	Z	E	T
C	L	F	A	J	G	G	S	E	F	N	P

Elevator   Eleven   Emerald   Emotion   Energy

Engineer   English   Envelope   Equation   Equator

Erosion   Erratic   Europe

Name: _____

Date: _____

Unit 17 Spelling

Circle the correct spelling for each word.

	A	B	C	D
1.	Elevator	Ellevatur	Elevatur	Ellevator
2.	Ellaven	Elaven	Eleven	Elleven
3.	Emerald	Emerrild	Emerrald	Emerild
4.	Emotion	Emotoin	Emottion	Emottoin
5.	Enargy	Energy	Enarrgy	Enerrgy
6.	Engineer	Enganer	Enginer	Enginear
7.	Engllash	Englash	English	Engllish
8.	Envelupe	Envelope	Envellope	Envellupe
9.	Equatoin	Equattion	Equattoin	Equation
10.	Eqauttor	Eqautor	Equator	Equattor
11.	Errosion	Erosion	Erosoin	Errosoin
12.	Erratac	Eratic	Eratac	Erratic
13.	Eorope	Eorrope	Eurrope	Europe

Write four sentences using as many words from your spelling list as you can. Underline the spelling words.

1. ....

2. ....

3. ....

4. ....

With permission Use an old magazine, newspaper or junk mail and find as many of your words in this unit you can (or the letters that make up your word). Cut it out, use a glue stick and paste it on your paper here.

Spelling Test

Your Answers	Correct Spelling If Incorrect
1	1
2	2
3	3
4	4
5	5
6	6
7	7
8	8
9	9
10	10
11	11
12	12
13	13
14	14
15	15
16	16
17	17
18	18
19	19
20	20

Unit 18 Unscramble

Let's put your puzzle solving skills to the test. Try unscrambling the words using the words in the box.

Explain	Figure	Exercise	Extend	Field	Evil
Everything	Except	Fault	Fifteen	Factory	Executive
Fifty	Fatal				

1. EVRYEINTHG   _ v _ _ y _ _ _ _ g

2. IVLE   E _ _ _

3. ETEPXC   _ x _ _ p _

4. TUVXEICEE   E x _ _ _ _ _ _ _

5. EEIESXCR   _ x _ _ _ i _ _

6. NEXLIAP   _ _ _ l a _ _

7. EDXENT   _ _ _ e _ d

8. OFRTYAC   F _ c _ _ _ _

9. LFATA   _ a _ _ _

10. TLFAU   _ a _ _ _

11. DIFEL   _ i _ _ _

12. FEFTNEI   _ _ _ t e _ _

13. FIFYT   _ _ _ t _

14. RFEUIG   _ i _ _ r _

Write a definition for each word. Underline the spelling words.

....

....

....

....

....

....

Unit 18 Wordsearch

Search the words from the given list below. Words can be across, down, diagonally and spread out.

R	N	V	J	H	D	N	E	T	X	E	P
O	U	N	E	E	T	F	I	F	R	I	A
O	G	J	Q	Y	L	Y	A	U	Z	L	P
R	K	B	S	J	U	D	G	T	C	A	E
F	M	Q	M	P	A	I	D	N	A	D	X
O	E	E	F	I	F	T	Y	J	X	L	E
S	Q	W	X	E	I	A	P	P	D	T	R
L	C	B	U	P	E	W	C	E	Y	B	C
W	L	E	V	I	L	R	E	T	C	U	I
C	E	G	H	H	D	A	N	R	O	X	S
T	E	X	E	C	U	T	I	V	E	R	E
E	V	E	R	Y	T	H	I	N	G	K	Y

Everything	Evil	Except	Executive	Exercise
Explain	Extend	Factory	Fatal	Fault
Field	Fifteen	Fifty	Figure	

Unit 18 Spelling

Circle the correct spelling for each word.

	A	**B**	**C**	**D**
1.	Everrything	Everything	Everrythang	Everythang
2.	Eval	Evill	Evil	Evall
3.	Exseptt	Except	Exceptt	Exsept
4.	Execottive	Executtive	Execotive	Executive
5.	Exerrcice	Exercise	Exercice	Exerrcise
6.	Explain	Expllian	Expllain	Explian
7.	Extend	Extand	Exttend	Exttand
8.	Facttury	Facttory	Factury	Factory
9.	Fattal	Fatal	Fital	Fittal
10.	Fault	Faullt	Fualt	Fuallt
11.	Feilld	Feild	Fielld	Field
12.	Fifteen	Fiften	Fiphten	Fiftean
13.	Fiffty	Fifty	Fiphfty	Fiphty
14.	Figore	Figure	Figorre	Figurre

Write four sentences using as many words from your spelling list as you can. Underline the spelling words.

1. ....

2. ....

3. ....

4. ....

With permission Use an old magazine, newspaper or junk mail and find as many of your words in this unit you can (or the letters that make up your word). Cut it out, use a glue stick and paste it on your paper here.

Spelling Test

Your Answers	Correct Spelling If Incorrect
1	1
2	2
3	3
4	4
5	5
6	6
7	7
8	8
9	9
10	10
11	11
12	12
13	13
14	14
15	15
16	16
17	17
18	18
19	19
20	20

Unit 19 Unscramble

Name: _____

Date: _____

Let's put your puzzle solving skills to the test. Try unscrambling the words using the words in the box.

Filled	Fixture	Force	Freckle	Finger	Forward
Flamingo	Frame	Forty	Fragile	Flooding	Fossil
Flasher	Footprint	Fourteen	Finally		

1. EILFLD   _ _ _ _ e d

2. IAFYLLN   _ i _ _ _ l _

3. EFNGIR   _ _ _ g _ r

4. FIUXRET   _ i _ _ _ e

5. IFGAOLMN   F _ _ _ i _ _ _

6. HSELFRA   _ _ _ _ h e _

7. ILFNOGDO   _ _ o _ _ _ _ g

8. POFTIOTRN   _ o _ _ _ _ n _

9. FEORC   F _ _ _ _

10. ROYFT   F _ _ _ _

11. OFWRARD   F _ _ _ _ _ d

12. SIFOLS   F _ _ s _ _

13. EOTEURFN   _ o _ _ _ _ _ n

14. AREGLIF   _ _ a _ _ _ e

15. FMAER   _ _ _ _ e

16. LFEKREC   _ _ _ _ k _ e

Write a definition for each word. Underline the spelling words.

....

....

....

....

Unit 19 Wordsearch

Search the words from the given list below. Words can be across, down, diagonally and spread out.

C	V	D	E	L	L	I	F	G	N	O	T
G	N	I	D	O	O	L	F	F	E	J	H
E	D	S	K	B	A	Y	I	E	E	E	O
C	E	I	F	M	T	N	X	L	T	F	M
R	L	Z	I	R	G	M	T	A	R	O	D
O	I	N	O	E	A	J	U	S	U	R	U
F	G	F	R	V	K	M	R	J	O	W	F
O	A	H	E	L	K	C	E	R	F	A	O
S	R	E	H	S	A	L	F	I	H	R	I
S	F	O	O	T	P	R	I	N	T	D	A
I	O	R	A	Y	L	L	A	N	I	F	I
L	I	N	Z	F	R	J	X	S	G	S	Y

Filled	Finally	Finger	Fixture	Flamingo
Flasher	Flooding	Footprint	Force	Forty
Forward	Fossil	Fourteen	Fragile	Frame
Freckle				

Unit 19 Spelling

Circle the correct spelling for each word.

	A	B	C	D
1.	Filew	Filled	Faled	Falled
2.	Fanally	Finaly	Fanaly	Finally
3.	Fingerr	Finjer	Finjerr	Finger
4.	Fixtture	Fixture	Fixttore	Fixtore
5.	Flamingo	Flamingu	Fllamingo	Fllamingu
6.	Flasher	Flisher	Fllisher	Fllasher
7.	Floding	Fluding	Flooding	Flouding
8.	Footprint	Fotprint	Futprint	Foutprint
9.	Forrse	Forse	Force	Forrce
10.	Forrty	Furty	Furrty	Forty
11.	Forward	Forrward	Furrward	Furward
12.	Fossil	Fosil	Foussil	Fousil
13.	Fourten	Fourtean	Foorten	Fourteen
14.	Fragile	Frragile	Frradgile	Fradgile
15.	Frime	Frrime	Frame	Frrame
16.	Frreckle	Frekle	Frrekle	Freckle

Write four sentences using as many words from your spelling list as you can. Underline the spelling words.

1. ....

2. ....

3. ....

4. ....

With permission Use an old magazine, newspaper or junk mail and find as many of your words in this unit you can (or the letters that make up your word). Cut it out, use a glue stick and paste it on your paper here.

Spelling Test

Your Answers		Correct Spelling If Incorrect	
1		1	
2		2	
3		3	
4		4	
5		5	
6		6	
7		7	
8		8	
9		9	
10		10	
11		11	
12		12	
13		13	
14		14	
15		15	
16		16	
17		17	
18		18	
19		19	
20		20	

Unit 20 Unscramble

Let's put your puzzle solving skills to the test. Try unscrambling the words using the words in the box.

Fragile	Frame	Finally	Forward	Footprint	Fixture
Filled	Flamingo	Force	Finger	Flooding	Forty
Freckle	Flasher	Fourteen	Fossil		

1. ILFELD   F _ _ _ e _

2. AIYNLLF   _ _ _ a _ l _

3. INGREF   F i _ _ _ _

4. FRTXUEI   F _ _ _ _ r _

5. MGAINFLO   _ _ a _ _ n _ _

6. LFESRAH   _ _ _ s _ _ r

7. OFDLNIOG   _ _ o _ _ _ _ g

8. NPTOFORIT   _ _ _ t _ _ _ n _

9. ECORF   _ _ _ c _

10. OTFRY   _ _ _ _ y

11. FORWADR   _ _ _ w a _ _

12. SLSIFO   _ o _ _ _ l

13. ONETFURE   _ _ _ _ t _ _ n

14. FIRAGLE   F _ _ _ i _ _

15. FRMAE   _ _ _ m _

16. FREKCLE   F r _ _ _ _ _

Write a definition for each word. Underline the spelling words.

....

....

....

....

....

Unit 20 Wordsearch

Search the words from the given list below. Words can be across, down, diagonally and spread out.

```
I  E  Z  C  C  X  G  A  W  C  N  Q
T  Z  G  G  G  O  L  D  E  N  G  Q
E  I  O  B  G  G  A  V  K  T  E  D
R  L  R  G  O  E  C  Y  M  G  R  D
U  A  I  A  O  N  I  I  A  V  B  N
T  R  L  R  S  E  E  B  N  O  I  E
I  E  L  L  E  R  R  F  Q  E  L  I
N  N  A  I  G  A  D  G  E  T  Z  R
R  E  B  C  G  T  C  H  S  E  R  F
U  G  L  O  B  E  V  O  O  D  Z  W
F  H  U  O  R  E  H  S  E  R  F  P
N  L  T  X  Y  G  A  L  L  O  N  I
```

Fresh	Fresher	Friend	Furniture	Gadget
Gallon	Garbage	Garlic	Generalize	Generate
Gerbil	Ghost	Glacier	Globe	Goal
Golden	Goose	Gorilla		

Unit 20 Spelling

Circle the correct spelling for each word.

	A	B	C	D
1.	Fresh	Frash	Frrash	Frresh
2.	Frresher	Fresher	Frasher	Frrasher
3.	Frriend	Frreind	Friend	Freind
4.	Furniture	Forniture	Forrniture	Furrniture
5.	Gagett	Gadget	Gadgett	Gaget
6.	Gallon	Galun	Gallun	Galon
7.	Garrbage	Garbadge	Garbage	Garrbadge
8.	Garlac	Garrlic	Garlic	Garrlac
9.	Generralaze	Generalize	Generalaze	Generralize
10.	Generrite	Generate	Generrate	Generite
11.	Gerbil	Gerrbal	Gerbal	Gerrbil
12.	Ghoust	Ghosst	Ghost	Ghousst
13.	Glacier	Glaceir	Gllaceir	Gllacier
14.	Glube	Globe	Gllube	Gllobe
15.	Goall	Gual	Guall	Goal
16.	Gullden	Gulhen	Gollden	Golden
17.	Gose	Gots	Gouse	Goose
18.	Gorilla	Gorila	Gurila	Gurilla

Write four sentences using as many words from your spelling list as you can. Underline the spelling words.

1. ....

2. ....

With permission Use an old magazine, newspaper or junk mail and find as many of your words in this unit you can (or the letters that make up your word). Cut it out, use a glue stick and paste it on your paper here.

Spelling Test

Your Answers		Correct Spelling If Incorrect	
1		1	
2		2	
3		3	
4		4	
5		5	
6		6	
7		7	
8		8	
9		9	
10		10	
11		11	
12		12	
13		13	
14		14	
15		15	
16		16	
17		17	
18		18	
19		19	
20		20	

Unit 21 Unscramble

Let's put your puzzle solving skills to the test. Try unscrambling the words using the words in the box.

Guest	Harbor	Habitat	Happened	Gusher	Heart
Heaven	Habit	Hemisphere	Heard	Half	Hammer
Heavy	Grapefruit				

1. EFRRTGPIAU   G _ _ p _ _ _ _ i _

2. STGUE   _ _ _ s _

3. URSHEG   _ u _ _ _ r

4. BAIHT   _ _ b _ _

5. HTITBAA   H _ _ _ _ _ t

6. FHAL   H _ _ _

7. RMAMHE   H _ m _ _ _

8. ADPEEPNH   _ a _ p _ _ _ _

9. AHBRRO   _ a _ b _ _

10. AHRED   _ e _ _ _

11. AEHRT   H _ _ _ _

12. VEEHNA   _ _ _ v _ n

13. HVEYA   _ _ _ _ y

14. SHEPEIHEMR   _ _ _ i s _ h _ _ _

Write a definition for each word. Underline the spelling words.

....

....

....

....

....

Unit 21 Wordsearch

Name: _____

Date: _____

Search the words from the given list below. Words can be across, down, diagonally and spread out.

```
T  H  U  N  C  Q  M  E  J  T  P  C
K  G  N  M  F  N  H  Y  S  M  D  W
W  U  R  L  Y  G  E  Q  C  Z  B  H
I  S  A  A  O  D  J  V  F  V  I  E
G  H  A  M  P  D  R  T  A  W  H  M
H  E  T  R  A  E  H  D  I  E  R  I
G  R  T  Q  M  N  F  A  A  B  H  S
U  C  T  M  F  E  A  R  R  N  A  P
E  Z  A  X  W  P  D  F  U  B  N  H
S  H  G  G  W  P  A  Y  K  I  O  E
T  A  T  I  B  A  H  J  J  V  T  R
N  Y  V  A  E  H  W  L  V  J  F  E
```

Grapefruit	Guest	Gusher	Habit	Habitat
Half	Hammer	Happened	Harbor	Heard
Heart	Heaven	Heavy	Hemisphere	

Unit 21 Spelling

Circle the correct spelling for each word.

	A	B	C	D
1.	Grapephruit	Grapefruit	Grrapefruit	Grrapephruit
2.	Guest	Guesst	Goest	Guesct
3.	Gussher	Gosher	Guscher	Gusher
4.	Habatt	Habit	Habat	Habitt
5.	Habattat	Habitat	Habittat	Habatat
6.	Hallf	Half	Halph	Hallph
7.	Himmer	Himer	Hamer	Hammer
8.	Hipened	Hippened	Hapened	Happened
9.	Harrbur	Harbur	Harrbor	Harbor
10.	Hearrd	Haerrd	Haerd	Heard
11.	Haerrt	Heart	Hearrt	Haert
12.	Heaven	Haeven	Heiven	Hieven
13.	Heavy	Haevy	Heivy	Hievy
14.	Hemisphere	Hemisfere	Hemissphere	Hemiscphere

Write four sentences using as many words from your spelling list as you can. Underline the spelling words.

1. ....

2. ....

3. ....

4. ....

With permission Use an old magazine, newspaper or junk mail and find as many of your words in this unit you can (or the letters that make up your word). Cut it out, use a glue stick and paste it on your paper here.

Spelling Test

Your Answers	
1	
2	
3	
4	
5	
6	
7	
8	
9	
10	
11	
12	
13	
14	
15	
16	
17	
18	
19	
20	

Correct Spelling If Incorrect	
1	
2	
3	
4	
5	
6	
7	
8	
9	
10	
11	
12	
13	
14	
15	
16	
17	
18	
19	
20	

Unit 22 Unscramble

Let's put your puzzle solving skills to the test. Try unscrambling the words using the words in the box.

Hermit	Illustrate	Hostile	Herd	Hotel	Illusion
Homework	Iceberg	Immature	Imitate	Hundredths	Husband
Illegal	Image	Igloo			

1. HRED   _ _ r _

2. MTIRHE   H _ r _ _ _

3. ROMKWHEO   _ _ m _ w _ _ _

4. ILHSETO   H _ _ _ i _ _

5. OLHET   _ _ t _ _

6. HDNHDSUETR   _ _ _ _ _ _ _ t h s

7. SNABDHU   _ _ _ _ a _ d

8. EBGICRE   _ _ _ _ e r _

9. LIOOG   _ g _ _ _

10. GELLLIA   _ _ l _ _ a _

11. NILUISOL   l _ _ u _ _ _ _

12. ESTULIARLT   l _ _ u _ _ _ _ _ e

13. IAMEG   _ _ _ _ e

14. AITEIMT   _ _ _ t a _ _

15. TIMMRUEA   _ m _ _ t _ _ _

Write a definition for each word. Underline the spelling words.

....

....

....

....

....

Unit 22 Wordsearch

Search the words from the given list below. Words can be across, down, diagonally and spread out.

D	E	L	I	T	S	O	H	S	Q	J	C
N	L	S	I	M	M	A	T	U	R	E	N
A	G	I	T	D	A	U	P	M	S	T	B
B	G	I	L	L	E	G	A	L	H	A	X
S	H	O	O	L	G	I	E	U	T	R	R
U	O	W	O	L	U	E	U	W	D	T	W
H	M	W	E	E	I	S	F	T	E	S	P
O	E	T	A	T	I	M	I	J	R	U	O
P	W	R	A	O	G	M	C	O	D	L	C
G	O	Z	D	H	R	J	I	X	N	L	E
X	R	I	C	E	B	E	R	G	U	I	U
V	K	I	H	D	S	B	T	O	H	L	W

Herd	Hermit	Homework	Hostile	Hotel
Hundredths	Husband	Iceberg	Igloo	Illegal
Illusion	Illustrate	Image	Imitate	Immature

With permission Use an old magazine, newspaper or junk mail and find as many of your words in this unit you can (or the letters that make up your word). Cut it out, use a glue stick and paste it on your paper here.

Spelling Test

Your Answers		Correct Spelling If Incorrect	
1		1	
2		2	
3		3	
4		4	
5		5	
6		6	
7		7	
8		8	
9		9	
10		10	
11		11	
12		12	
13		13	
14		14	
15		15	
16		16	
17		17	
18		18	
19		19	
20		20	

Unit 23 Unscramble

Name: _____

Date: _____

Let's put your puzzle solving skills to the test. Try unscrambling the words using the words in the box.

Immigrant	Interest	Include	Invasion	Inside	Intersecting
Infection	Instruments	Invention	Instead	Inflation	Inspection

1. INARIMGTM   _ m m _ _ _ _ _ _

2. EIULNCD   _ n _ _ _ d _

3. FINTNCIEO   _ _ _ _ t _ o _

4. ALTINNOFI   I _ _ _ _ _ _ _ n

5. IEDSIN   I _ s _ _ _

6. EICNISPNTO   _ _ _ p e c _ _ _ _

7. ADNTESI   _ _ _ t _ _ d

8. RENUMNSTSTI   _ _ _ _ _ u _ e _ _ s

9. ITRNTSEE   _ _ t _ _ _ s _

10. SCEGEIITTNRN   I _ _ _ _ _ _ c t _ _ _

11. VIOSNINA   _ _ _ _ s _ o _

12. IVTINENON   _ _ v e _ _ _ _ _

Write a definition for each word. Underline the spelling words.

_____

_____

_____

_____

Unit 23 Wordsearch

Search the words from the given list below. Words can be across, down, diagonally and spread out.

G	Z	I	I	Y	R	L	J	H	Q	I	E
N	S	B	N	N	C	D	F	N	E	N	F
I	L	T	S	F	S	A	F	F	O	F	I
T	S	S	T	Y	E	I	X	E	J	L	N
C	O	E	E	O	L	C	D	T	O	A	V
E	Q	R	A	H	V	U	T	E	H	T	E
S	N	E	D	T	L	Y	I	I	N	I	N
R	K	T	A	C	Z	K	Z	H	O	O	T
E	U	N	N	N	O	I	S	A	V	N	I
T	W	I	M	M	I	G	R	A	N	T	O
N	W	I	N	S	P	E	C	T	I	O	N
I	I	N	S	T	R	U	M	E	N	T	S

Immigrant	Include	Infection	Inflation
Inside	Inspection	Instead	Instruments
Interest	Intersecting	Invasion	Invention

Unit 23 Spelling

Circle the correct spelling for each word.

	A	B	C	D
1.	Imigrant	Imagrant	Immigrant	Immagrant
2.	Incllude	Inclode	Include	Incllode
3.	Inffection	Infectoin	Inffectoin	Infection
4.	Inflation	Infflation	Infflatoin	Inflatoin
5.	Inscide	Inside	Insside	Insade
6.	Inspection	Insspectoin	Insspection	Inspectoin
7.	Instead	Insstead	Instaed	Insstaed
8.	Instruments	Insstruments	Instrunments	Insstrunments
9.	Intarest	Interest	Inttarest	Intterest
10.	Inttersecting	Intersecting	Inttercecting	Intercecting
11.	Invasion	Invassoin	Invasoin	Invassion
12.	Inventtoin	Invention	Inventoin	Inventtion

Write four sentences using as many words from your spelling list as you can. Underline the spelling words.

1. ....

2. ....

3. ....

4. ....

With permission Use an old magazine, newspaper or junk mail and find as many of your words in this unit you can (or the letters that make up your word). Cut it out, use a glue stick and paste it on your paper here.

Spelling Test

Your Answers		Correct Spelling If Incorrect	
1		1	
2		2	
3		3	
4		4	
5		5	
6		6	
7		7	
8		8	
9		9	
10		10	
11		11	
12		12	
13		13	
14		14	
15		15	
16		16	
17		17	
18		18	
19		19	
20		20	

Unit 24 Unscramble

Let's put your puzzle solving skills to the test. Try unscrambling the words using the words in the box.

Island	Judicial	Jungle	Joined	Keyboard	Kangaroo
Invitation	Itself	Kept	Irritation	Jewel	Juvenile

1. VANITNITOI   _ n _ _ _ a _ i _ _

2. IANRTIITOR   I _ _ _ _ _ t _ o _

3. SADLIN   _ _ l _ n _

4. SIELTF   I _ s _ _ _

5. WELEJ   _ _ _ _ l

6. JIDENO   _ o i _ _ _

7. UIDLCIAJ   J _ d _ _ _ _ _

8. JNGLEU   _ _ n _ l _

9. IUEJLEVN   _ _ _ e _ _ _ e

10. OGAKOANR   _ _ n _ a _ _ _

11. ETKP   _ e _ _

12. YBREAKDO   _ _ _ _ _ a r _

Write a definition for each word. Underline the spelling words.

_____

_____

_____

_____

_____

_____

_____

Unit 24 Wordsearch

Search the words from the given list below. Words can be across, down, diagonally and spread out.

A	U	U	L	O	A	Q	T	X	Y	J	I
T	T	P	E	K	F	U	O	Z	U	M	R
B	Y	D	V	S	A	W	A	V	C	C	R
I	T	S	E	L	F	N	E	D	P	D	I
M	D	G	C	N	G	N	G	R	N	C	T
V	R	J	U	D	I	C	I	A	L	M	A
J	U	N	G	L	E	O	L	O	R	E	T
I	Y	V	E	G	S	S	J	B	H	O	I
S	J	C	H	B	I	A	A	Y	W	M	O
G	N	A	D	F	L	E	W	E	J	P	N
T	Z	O	I	J	Y	W	O	K	Q	F	R
R	H	I	N	V	I	T	A	T	I	O	N

Invitation	Irritation	Island	Itself
Jewel	Joined	Judicial	Jungle
Juvenile	Kangaroo	Kept	Keyboard

Unit 24 Spelling

Circle the correct spelling for each word.

	A	B	C	D
1.	Invitatoin	Invitation	Invittation	Invittatoin
2.	Iritatoin	Irritation	Irritatoin	Iritation
3.	Iscland	Island	Islind	Issland
4.	Itself	Itcelf	Ittcelf	Ittself
5.	Jewel	Jewell	Jawel	Jawell
6.	Joine	Joined	Juined	Jioned
7.	Judiciall	Judicial	Judicail	Judicaill
8.	Junglle	Jonglle	Jungle	Jongle
9.	Juvenille	Juvenile	Jovenile	Jovenille
10.	Kangarou	Kangaroo	Kangaru	Kangaro
11.	Keptt	Kapt	Kaptt	Kept
12.	Kayboard	Kayboarrd	Keyboarrd	Keyboard

Write four sentences using as many words from your spelling list as you can. Underline the spelling words.

1. ....

2. ....

3. ....

4. ....

With permission Use an old magazine, newspaper or junk mail and find as many of your words in this unit you can (or the letters that make up your word). Cut it out, use a glue stick and paste it on your paper here.

Spelling Test

Your Answers
1
2
3
4
5
6
7
8
9
10
11
12
13
14
15
16
17
18
19
20

Correct Spelling If Incorrect
1
2
3
4
5
6
7
8
9
10
11
12
13
14
15
16
17
18
19
20

Unit 25 Unscramble

Let's put your puzzle solving skills to the test. Try unscrambling the words using the words in the box.

Language	Lettuce	Ledge	Knuckle	Latitude	Kingdom
Lecture	Landscape	Knight	Legislative	Kilometer	Lemon
Listening	Leisure				

1. LKTERMEOI   _ i _ o _ _ _ _ _

2. DNOIKGM   _ _ n _ _ o _

3. GIKTHN   _ n _ _ h _

4. CUKLEKN   _ _ _ c k _ _

5. NLAESPCAD   L a _ _ _ _ _ _ _

6. AGGNULEA   L _ _ _ _ _ g _

7. LUIADETT   _ a _ _ _ _ _ e

8. ECERUTL   L _ _ _ _ r _

9. EELGD   _ _ d _ _

10. VLLTAGEISIE   _ _ g _ s _ _ _ _ _ e

11. SLUEREI   _ e _ _ u _ _

12. NELMO   _ _ _ o _

13. TETCULE   L _ t _ _ _ _

14. NLSGTIIEN   _ _ _ t _ n _ _ _

Write a definition for each word. Underline the spelling words.

....

....

....

....

....

Unit 25 Wordsearch

Name: _____

Date: _____

Search the words from the given list below. Words can be across, down, diagonally and spread out.

P	S	L	I	S	T	E	N	I	N	G	U
E	F	E	P	A	C	S	D	N	A	L	J
O	A	G	V	E	L	K	C	U	N	K	V
G	B	I	L	E	C	T	U	R	E	K	U
I	M	S	L	E	Q	U	I	E	R	G	X
M	G	L	C	A	M	T	T	Z	O	U	H
O	L	A	X	H	T	O	S	T	L	Y	E
D	S	T	T	H	G	I	N	K	E	W	G
G	K	I	L	O	M	E	T	E	R	L	D
N	P	V	P	L	A	N	G	U	A	G	E
I	W	E	J	U	Q	D	K	U	D	G	L
K	J	T	G	L	E	I	S	U	R	E	M

Kilometer	Kingdom	Knight	Knuckle	Landscape
Language	Latitude	Lecture	Ledge	Legislative
Leisure	Lemon	Lettuce	Listening	

Unit 25 Spelling

Name: _____

Date: _____

Circle the correct spelling for each word.

	A	B	C	D
1.	Kilumeter	Killumeter	Kilometer	Killometer
2.	Kangdm	Kingdum	Kingdom	Kingdm
3.	Knaghtt	Knightt	Knaght	Knight
4.	Knuklle	Knucklle	Knuckle	Knukle
5.	Landsssape	Landssape	Landsscape	Landscape
6.	Langauge	Languadge	Language	Langaudge
7.	Lattitude	Latitude	Lattitode	Latitode
8.	Lecttore	Lectture	Lectore	Lecture
9.	Ledje	Lede	Ledge	Ladj
10.	Legislative	Legaslative	Legisclative	Legisslative
11.	Leisure	Liesure	Liessure	Leissure
12.	Lamn	Lemn	Lemon	Lemun
13.	Letuse	Lettuse	Lettuce	Letuce
14.	Lastening	Listening	Lisstening	Lisctening

Write four sentences using as many words from your spelling list as you can. Underline the spelling words.

1. ....

2. ....

3. ....

4. ....

With permission Use an old magazine, newspaper or junk mail and find as many of your words in this unit you can (or the letters that make up your word). Cut it out, use a glue stick and paste it on your paper here.

Spelling Test

Your Answers	Correct Spelling If Incorrect
1	1
2	2
3	3
4	4
5	5
6	6
7	7
8	8
9	9
10	10
11	11
12	12
13	13
14	14
15	15
16	16
17	17
18	18
19	19
20	20

Unit 26 Unscramble

Let's put your puzzle solving skills to the test. Try unscrambling the words using the words in the box.

Medium	Magnetic	Liter	Member	Luggage	Machine
Marble	Locally	Memory	Maybe	Lodge	Literature
Longitude	Mental	Mathematics	Lower		

1. LERTI   _ _ _ _ r

2. RUTEETIALR   _ _ _ e _ a t _ _ _

3. LLOALCY   _ o c _ _ _ _

4. OGEDL   _ _ _ _ e

5. DTIEGLUON   L _ _ _ _ _ _ d _

6. OWERL   L _ _ _ _

7. EAGGLUG   _ u g _ _ _ _

8. HNECIAM   _ _ _ h i _ _

9. GMEACNIT   _ a _ _ _ _ i _

10. LEMBAR   M _ _ _ l _

11. CAMITSTAHEM   _ a _ _ _ m _ _ i _ _

12. YABEM   _ _ _ _ e

13. DIUMEM   _ _ _ i _ m

14. EBMRME   _ e _ _ _ r

15. MERYMO   _ e _ o _ _

16. EANLMT   _ e n _ _ _

Write a definition for each word. Underline the spelling words.

....

....

....

....

Name: _____

Date: _____

Unit 26 Wordsearch

Search the words from the given list below. Words can be across, down, diagonally and spread out.

```
F  M  A  R  B  L  E  H  H  B  E  Y
E  D  U  T  I  G  N  O  L  A  G  V
M  E  N  I  H  C  A  M  D  N  D  P
P  H  U  C  D  M  M  P  H  M  O  B
L  M  A  Y  B  E  R  E  W  O  L  L
V  V  R  F  A  M  M  R  N  U  T  O
W  C  E  M  K  B  K  O  G  T  E  C
B  D  T  F  Q  E  K  G  E  Q  A  A
X  L  I  T  E  R  A  T  U  R  E  L
X  D  L  M  A  G  N  E  T  I  C  L
H  E  S  M  E  M  O  R  Y  Z  A  Y
S  C  I  T  A  M  E  H  T  A  M  I
```

Liter	Literature	Locally	Lodge	Longitude
Lower	Luggage	Machine	Magnetic	Marble
Mathematics	Maybe	Medium	Member	Memory
Mental				

Unit 26 Spelling

Circle the correct spelling for each word.

	A	B	C	D
1.	Latjer	Latvr	Liter	Linjer
2.	Literature	Literatore	Litteratore	Litterature
3.	Lucaly	Localy	Locally	Lucally
4.	Lodge	Lude	Ldde	Lodje
5.	Longittude	Longitude	Longittode	Longitode
6.	Lower	Luwer	Lowerr	Luwerr
7.	Lugage	Luggage	Luggadge	Lugadge
8.	Machine	Machei	Machie	Machane
9.	Madgnetic	Madgnettic	Magnetic	Magnettic
10.	Mirble	Marrble	Mirrble	Marble
11.	Matthematacs	Mathematacs	Matthematics	Mathematics
12.	Miybe	Mayb	Meybe	Maybe
13.	Medam	Medim	Medium	Mediom
14.	Memberr	Mamber	Mamberr	Member
15.	Memorry	Memory	Memurry	Memury
16.	Mentil	Mental	Menttal	Menttil

Write four sentences using as many words from your spelling list as you can. Underline the spelling words.

1. ....

2. ....

3. ....

4. ....

With permission Use an old magazine, newspaper or junk mail and find as many of your words in this unit you can (or the letters that make up your word). Cut it out, use a glue stick and paste it on your paper here.

Spelling Test

Your Answers	Correct Spelling If Incorrect
1	1
2	2
3	3
4	4
5	5
6	6
7	7
8	8
9	9
10	10
11	11
12	12
13	13
14	14
15	15
16	16
17	17
18	18
19	19
20	20

Unit 27 Unscramble

Let's put your puzzle solving skills to the test. Try unscrambling the words using the words in the box.

Moment	Mobile	Mistook	Metal	Method	Metaphor
Moisture	Mitten	Monitor	Minus	Millimeter	Mixture
Miniature	Miner	Merit	Mercy		

1. ECYMR   _ _ _ _ y

2. MIERT   _ _ _ i _

3. ATELM   _ e _ _ _

4. TPRHOAME   _ e _ _ _ o _

5. ODTMEH   _ _ t h _ _

6. EIMIMTRLLE   _ _ l _ _ _ _ t e _

7. MNEIR   _ _ n _ _

8. UENIMRTIA   _ _ _ _ _ _ u _ e

9. MNIUS   _ i _ _ _

10. OMKOSIT   _ i _ _ _ o _

11. ETINTM   _ _ t _ e _

12. URXMTIE   _ _ _ t u _ _

13. MEIOLB   M o _ _ _ _

14. IMOTUESR   _ o _ _ _ u _ _

15. MEOMNT   _ _ _ _ n t

16. OTMIRON   _ _ n _ _ _ r

Write a definition for each word. Underline the spelling words.

....

....

....

....

Unit 27 Wordsearch

Search the words from the given list below. Words can be across, down, diagonally and spread out.

L	M	I	L	L	I	M	E	T	E	R	N
S	O	O	E	R	U	T	A	I	N	I	M
U	I	I	B	Q	R	H	P	O	O	D	R
S	S	B	R	I	M	I	S	T	O	O	K
M	T	Y	N	O	L	J	N	W	H	H	X
N	U	O	L	A	T	E	M	P	S	T	V
W	R	P	M	B	M	I	A	O	U	E	A
S	E	R	C	O	S	T	N	F	N	M	V
N	X	Z	M	F	E	I	T	O	I	P	U
O	D	C	E	M	D	R	X	V	M	M	I
N	E	T	T	I	M	E	R	C	Y	S	U
E	R	U	T	X	I	M	I	N	E	R	O

Mercy	Merit	Metal	Metaphor	Method
Millimeter	Miner	Miniature	Minus	Mistook
Mitten	Mixture	Mobile	Moisture	Moment
Monitor				

Unit 27 Spelling

Circle the correct spelling for each word.

	A	B	C	D
1.	Mercy	Merrcy	Marrcy	Marcy
2.	Merat	Merrit	Merrat	Merit
3.	Metal	Mettil	Metil	Mettal
4.	Metaphor	Mettafor	Mettaphor	Metafor
5.	Metthud	Metthod	Methud	Method
6.	Milimeter	Mallimeter	Malimeter	Millimeter
7.	Miner	Maner	Minerr	Manerr
8.	Miniatture	Minaitture	Minaiture	Miniature
9.	Minusc	Minus	Minms	Minuss
10.	Mistook	Mistouk	Mistok	Mistock
11.	Maten	Mitten	Miten	Matten
12.	Mixtture	Mixture	Mixttore	Mixtore
13.	Mobille	Mubille	Mubile	Mobile
14.	Moisture	Miossture	Miosture	Moissture
15.	Monment	Monmentt	Moment	Momentt
16.	Monitor	Munitor	Monittor	Munittor

Write four sentences using as many words from your spelling list as you can. Underline the spelling words.

1. ....

2. ....

3. ....

4. ....

With permission Use an old magazine, newspaper or junk mail and find as many of your words in this unit you can (or the letters that make up your word). Cut it out, use a glue stick and paste it on your paper here.

Spelling Test

Your Answers		Correct Spelling If Incorrect	
1		1	
2		2	
3		3	
4		4	
5		5	
6		6	
7		7	
8		8	
9		9	
10		10	
11		11	
12		12	
13		13	
14		14	
15		15	
16		16	
17		17	
18		18	
19		19	
20		20	

Unit 28 Unscramble

Let's put your puzzle solving skills to the test. Try unscrambling the words using the words in the box.

Mute	Musket	Neither	Moody	Monster	Movement
Muffin	Nasal	Monkey	Negative	Mortal	Neighbor
Nail	Movie	Moraine			

1. NEYKMO   _ _ _ k e _

2. ERTMNSO   _ _ n s _ _ _

3. OOMDY   _ o _ _ _

4. ORNIAME   _ _ r a _ _ _

5. ATLOMR   M _ _ _ a _

6. MEEVMNOT   _ _ _ _ _ e _ t

7. IVEMO   _ o _ _ _

8. IMFNUF   _ _ _ f _ n

9. USTMKE   _ u _ k _ _

10. UEMT   _ _ t _

11. NLIA   _ _ i _

12. LANSA   _ _ _ _ l

13. AETEVNIG   N _ _ _ t _ _ _

14. IHBRONEG   _ _ _ _ h _ _ r

15. EREHTNI   _ _ _ _ h e _

Write a definition for each word. Underline the spelling words.

....

....

....

....

Unit 28 Wordsearch

Search the words from the given list below. Words can be across, down, diagonally and spread out.

R	B	T	V	Q	G	M	O	N	K	E	Y
E	V	I	T	A	G	E	N	V	Z	I	I
M	O	R	A	I	N	E	A	J	Q	F	W
M	Y	V	M	I	E	T	I	I	N	J	S
O	B	E	F	T	U	N	L	Z	A	U	F
V	F	F	U	S	Q	A	T	N	O	V	J
E	U	M	O	N	S	T	E	R	I	X	B
M	O	R	T	A	L	I	K	I	V	M	O
E	N	H	N	P	T	I	S	C	V	O	A
N	F	B	N	H	J	Y	U	W	M	O	C
T	W	S	E	I	O	H	M	H	S	D	M
H	M	R	O	B	H	G	I	E	N	Y	P

Monkey	Monster	Moody	Moraine	Mortal
Movement	Movie	Muffin	Musket	Mute
Nail	Nasal	Negative	Neighbor	Neither

Unit 28 Spelling

Circle the correct spelling for each word.

	A	B	C	D
1.	Monckey	Monckay	Monkey	Monkay
2.	Munstdr	Monster	Monscter	Monsster
3.	Mudy	Moudy	Moody	Mody
4.	Morriane	Morraine	Moriane	Moraine
5.	Murrtal	Morrtal	Mortal	Murtal
6.	Movement	Movementt	Movenmentt	Movenment
7.	Muvei	Movei	Movie	Muvie
8.	Muffin	Muphfin	Mufin	Muphin
9.	Mussket	Muscket	Muske	Musket
10.	Motve	Mute	Mutte	Myte
11.	Naill	Nial	Nail	Niall
12.	Nisal	Nasal	Nascal	Nassal
13.	Negative	Negattave	Negattive	Negatave
14.	Neighborr	Nieghbor	Neighbor	Nieghborr
15.	Neither	Niether	Neitther	Nietther

Write four sentences using as many words from your spelling list as you can. Underline the spelling words.

1. ....

2. ....

3. ....

4. ....

With permission Use an old magazine, newspaper or junk mail and find as many of your words in this unit you can (or the letters that make up your word). Cut it out, use a glue stick and paste it on your paper here.

Spelling Test

Your Answers		Correct Spelling If Incorrect	
1		1	
2		2	
3		3	
4		4	
5		5	
6		6	
7		7	
8		8	
9		9	
10		10	
11		11	
12		12	
13		13	
14		14	
15		15	
16		16	
17		17	
18		18	
19		19	
20		20	

Unit 29 Unscramble

Let's put your puzzle solving skills to the test. Try unscrambling the words using the words in the box.

Oval	Opinion	Orphan	Organism	Outside	Ninety
Occasion	Numerical	Nugget	Order	Origin	Neutral
Onion	Normal	Official	Orange		

1. EUNTLAR   _ _ u _ r _ _

2. INTYEN   _ i _ e _ _

3. ROANLM   _ _ r _ _ l

4. EUNGGT   _ _ g _ e _

5. NIEALUCMR   N _ m _ _ _ _ _ _

6. NACSICOO   _ _ _ _ _ i o _

7. IIOFCFAL   _ f f _ _ _ _ _

8. IOONN   _ _ i _ _

9. IPOIONN   O _ _ _ _ o _

10. AOGNRE   _ r a _ _ _

11. RORED   _ _ _ _ r

12. MNSRIAOG   O _ _ _ _ _ s _

13. ONRGII   _ _ _ g i _

14. HOPNAR   _ r _ _ a _

15. TSEOIUD   O _ _ s _ _ _

16. AOVL   _ _ _ l

Write a definition for each word. Underline the spelling words.

_____

_____

_____

_____

Unit 29 Wordsearch

Search the words from the given list below. Words can be across, down, diagonally and spread out.

Y	H	C	W	Y	T	E	N	I	N	N	X
E	K	H	E	Y	O	Z	V	B	U	I	X
Y	X	V	N	W	C	U	F	I	M	G	K
N	U	G	G	E	T	E	T	N	E	I	F
A	O	N	X	O	U	B	I	S	R	R	B
H	R	O	B	I	V	T	O	N	I	O	N
P	G	I	E	G	N	A	R	O	C	D	S
R	A	N	O	R	M	A	L	A	A	S	E
O	N	I	R	Q	Z	V	W	C	L	U	L
X	I	P	D	O	F	F	I	C	I	A	L
I	S	O	E	N	O	I	S	A	C	C	O
M	M	R	R	X	Y	I	S	S	X	R	E

Neutral	Ninety	Normal	Nugget	Numerical
Occasion	Official	Onion	Opinion	Orange
Order	Organism	Origin	Orphan	Outside
Oval				

Unit 29 Spelling

Name: _____

Date: _____

Circle the correct spelling for each word.

	A	**B**	**C**	**D**
1.	Neuttral	Neotral	Neottral	Neutral
2.	Nanetty	Ninetty	Ninety	Nanety
3.	Norrmal	Nurrmal	Nurmal	Normal
4.	Nugjet	Nujet	Nuget	Nugget
5.	Nomerical	Numerrical	Numerical	Nomerrical
6.	Occasoin	Occasion	Ocasion	Ocasoin
7.	Oficial	Officail	Oficail	Official
8.	Onoin	Onion	Onio	Oniun
9.	Opinio	Opinoin	Opiniun	Opinion
10.	Orrange	Orranje	Oranje	Orange
11.	Orrder	Order	Orrdar	Ordar
12.	Organasm	Organism	Orrganasm	Orrganism
13.	Oragin	Origin	Orrigin	Orragin
14.	Orphan	Orfan	Orrfan	Orrphan
15.	Oottside	Ootside	Outtside	Outside
16.	Ovill	Ovil	Oval	Ovall

Write four sentences using as many words from your spelling list as you can. Underline the spelling words.

1. ....

2. ....

3. ....

4. ....

With permission Use an old magazine, newspaper or junk mail and find as many of your words in this unit you can (or the letters that make up your word). Cut it out, use a glue stick and paste it on your paper here.

Spelling Test

Your Answers		Correct Spelling If Incorrect	
1		1	
2		2	
3		3	
4		4	
5		5	
6		6	
7		7	
8		8	
9		9	
10		10	
11		11	
12		12	
13		13	
14		14	
15		15	
16		16	
17		17	
18		18	
19		19	
20		20	

Unit 30 Unscramble

Let's put your puzzle solving skills to the test. Try unscrambling the words using the words in the box.

Partridge	Penguin	Pasture	Peanut	Owner	Participate
Package	Pattern	Oxen	Passage	Parallel	Parentheses
Pastel	Partial	Parsley			

1. WRNOE   O _ _ _ _

2. ONEX   _ x _ _

3. GCPAKEA   _ a c _ _ _ _

4. EAPLLRLA   _ a r _ _ _ _ _

5. HASETESNEPR   _ _ _ _ n _ h e _ _ _

6. SYEALPR   P _ _ _ _ _ y

7. LAPTRAI   _ _ _ _ i _ l

8. ITEIRAPCTAP   _ _ _ _ _ i _ _ _ a t _

9. GRRDIETPA   _ _ _ _ _ _ _ d g _

10. PSSEAAG   _ _ _ _ _ g e

11. PTASEL   P _ _ t _ _

12. SUEATRP   P _ s _ _ _ _

13. PENTRAT   _ _ _ _ e _ n

14. UETPAN   P _ _ _ _ t

15. IPENNGU   _ _ _ _ u _ n

Write a definition for each word. Underline the spelling words.

....

....

....

....

Unit 30 Wordsearch

Search the words from the given list below. Words can be across, down, diagonally and spread out.

S	E	S	E	H	T	N	E	R	A	P	D
Y	J	D	N	P	A	C	K	A	G	E	T
O	N	Y	R	E	N	W	O	K	T	V	V
Y	T	E	E	R	U	T	S	A	P	E	B
J	J	G	T	L	O	I	P	D	S	D	U
E	P	D	T	H	S	I	I	G	Y	F	D
G	A	I	A	P	C	R	C	P	F	Q	G
A	R	R	P	I	P	E	A	N	U	T	E
S	T	T	T	A	I	S	E	P	E	A	A
S	I	R	B	X	T	H	Y	K	Y	X	I
A	A	A	L	E	L	L	A	R	A	P	O
P	L	P	L	N	I	U	G	N	E	P	S

Owner	Oxen	Package	Parallel	Parentheses
Parsley	Partial	Participate	Partridge	Passage
Pastel	Pasture	Pattern	Peanut	Penguin

Unit 30 Spelling

Name: _____

Date: _____

Circle the correct spelling for each word.

	A	B	C	D
1.	Ownarr	Ownar	Ownerr	Owner
2.	Oxa	Oxan	Oxen	Oxn
3.	Packea	Package	Packadge	Packae
4.	Paralel	Piralel	Pirallel	Parallel
5.	Parrentheces	Parentheses	Parentheces	Parrentheses
6.	Parslay	Parrsley	Parsley	Parrslay
7.	Parrtial	Parrtail	Partial	Partail
8.	Partacipate	Participate	Parrticipate	Parrtacipate
9.	Parrtridge	Partridge	Parrtridje	Partridje
10.	Pasage	Passage	Passadge	Pasadge
11.	Pasctel	Passtel	Pastel	Pistel
12.	Pascture	Passture	Pastore	Pasture
13.	Pattern	Pittern	Pitern	Patern
14.	Peanut	Paenutt	Paenut	Peanutt
15.	Penguin	Pengoin	Pengon	Pengun

Write four sentences using as many words from your spelling list as you can. Underline the spelling words.

1. ....

2. ....

3. ....

4. ....

With permission Use an old magazine, newspaper or junk mail and find as many of your words in this unit you can (or the letters that make up your word). Cut it out, use a glue stick and paste it on your paper here.

Spelling Test

Your Answers	Correct Spelling If Incorrect
1	1
2	2
3	3
4	4
5	5
6	6
7	7
8	8
9	9
10	10
11	11
12	12
13	13
14	14
15	15
16	16
17	17
18	18
19	19
20	20

Unit 31 Unscramble

Let's put your puzzle solving skills to the test. Try unscrambling the words using the words in the box.

Perhaps	Pineapple	Pint	Piece	Phrase	Percussion
Pitcher	Percent	Pioneer	Perpendicular	Permanent	Perch
Perish	Plateau				

1. RPNTEEC   P _ _ _ _ _ t

2. HREPC   _ e _ _ _

3. NIUSSRPCOE   P e _ _ _ _ _ i _ _

4. RHPAESP   P e _ _ _ _ _

5. RSPEHI   P _ _ i _ _

6. EMRNATNEP   _ _ r _ _ _ _ _ t

7. LUEADPEPRNCRI   P _ _ p _ n _ _ _ _ _ _ _

8. PHRSAE   P _ r _ _ _

9. EIEPC   _ _ _ _ e

10. AENPIELPP   P _ _ _ _ _ _ _ e

11. PTIN   _ _ n _

12. REENPOI   _ _ o _ e _ _

13. CETRHIP   P _ _ c _ _ _

14. PTAALEU   P _ _ _ _ a _

Write a definition for each word. Underline the spelling words.

....

....

Unit 31 Wordsearch

Search the words from the given list below. Words can be across, down, diagonally and spread out.

X	F	Z	D	U	T	D	F	E	Q	D	D	Q	V	O	G
X	P	Z	M	T	O	Z	T	F	O	B	R	N	P	G	T
D	E	L	B	P	U	M	E	G	I	K	W	W	U	N	N
L	X	D	Y	E	C	E	I	P	X	K	S	E	E	P	J
P	R	P	E	R	C	U	S	S	I	O	N	C	B	I	T
A	M	E	C	P	S	N	P	G	V	Y	R	O	A	T	C
A	Q	T	E	E	A	H	E	S	S	E	H	H	M	C	K
M	T	N	E	N	A	M	R	E	P	E	R	I	S	H	F
C	J	B	T	D	O	C	C	S	H	A	U	B	P	E	B
U	W	T	N	I	P	I	H	Q	R	P	H	L	O	R	E
M	A	E	H	C	I	G	P	T	A	T	S	R	T	T	A
S	C	E	B	U	W	W	B	D	S	K	D	L	E	W	V
I	H	O	T	L	J	C	K	C	E	R	W	X	S	P	X
E	L	P	P	A	E	N	I	P	N	V	S	P	N	I	F
Q	T	X	F	R	L	V	S	L	R	V	K	S	S	R	B
Q	R	P	P	S	O	P	W	V	Q	C	O	J	C	Y	A

Percent	Perch	Percussion	Perhaps	Perish
Permanent	Perpendicular	Phrase	Piece	Pineapple
Pint	Pioneer	Pitcher	Plateau	

Unit 31 Spelling

Circle the correct spelling for each word.

	A	B	C	D
1.	Percent	Persent	Perrsent	Perrcent
2.	Parrch	Perch	Parck	Perrch
3.	Percussion	Percusion	Percussoin	Percusoin
4.	Perrhaps	Perrhips	Perhaps	Perhips
5.	Perash	Perish	Perrash	Perrish
6.	Perrmanent	Perminent	Perrminent	Permanent
7.	Perpendicular	Perpendicolar	Perrpendicular	Perrpendicolar
8.	Phrrace	Phrase	Phrace	Phrrase
9.	Piece	Peice	Piese	Pewse
10.	Pineaple	Pineapple	Pinaepple	Pinaeple
11.	Pamt	Pintt	Pint	Pantt
12.	Pioner	Pioneer	Poineer	Poiner
13.	Pittcher	Pitcher	Patlher	Pattcher
14.	Pllataeu	Pllateau	Plataeu	Plateau

Write four sentences using as many words from your spelling list as you can. Underline the spelling words.

1. ....

2. ....

3. ....

4. ....

With permission Use an old magazine, newspaper or junk mail and find as many of your words in this unit you can (or the letters that make up your word). Cut it out, use a glue stick and paste it on your paper here.

Spelling Test

	Your Answers
1	
2	
3	
4	
5	
6	
7	
8	
9	
10	
11	
12	
13	
14	
15	
16	
17	
18	
19	
20	

	Correct Spelling If Incorrect
1	
2	
3	
4	
5	
6	
7	
8	
9	
10	
11	
12	
13	
14	
15	
16	
17	
18	
19	
20	

Unit 32 Unscramble

Let's put your puzzle solving skills to the test. Try unscrambling the words using the words in the box.

Pollution	Poet	Poison	Polite	Population	Postal
Porch	Plenty	Portal	Porridge	Pleasure	Positive
Pledge	Plus				

1. ESUALPRE   _ l _ _ s _ _ _

8. UNTOLOPIL   _ o _ _ _ t _ _ _

2. PEELGD   P l _ _ _ _

9. ULINOAPPOT   _ _ _ _ _ _ t i _ n

3. TYNELP   _ _ _ n t _

10. PHROC   _ _ _ _ h

4. SUPL   _ _ _ s

11. ROIRGPED   _ _ r _ _ _ g _

5. TEOP   _ _ e _

12. APORLT   _ _ r _ a _

6. NOSIPO   _ o _ _ o _

13. STVOPIIE   P _ _ i _ _ _ _

7. EIOPLT   _ o l _ _ _

14. OSTLPA   _ o _ t _ _

Write a definition for each word. Underline the spelling words.

_____

_____

_____

_____

_____

Name: _____

Date: _____

Unit 32 Wordsearch

Search the words from the given list below. Words can be across, down, diagonally and spread out.

K T X E R U S A E L P N

S S H V Q L P E P I H Y

M X U C F O O B O Y Q U

U Z N L R P N O S I O P

P Z Y T P O R R I D G E

H W A K K L P J T V X J

J L T I K I Z G I J L V

F Y B Z O T D B V D A Y

E B A A J E P L E N T Y

L I G R P L E D G E S B

S N O I T U L L O P O Q

N O I T A L U P O P P U

Pleasure	Pledge	Plenty	Plus	Poet
Poison	Polite	Pollution	Population	Porch
Porridge	Portal	Positive	Postal	

Unit 32 Spelling

Name: _____

Date: _____

Circle the correct spelling for each word.

	A	B	C	D
1.	Pleasure	Plaesure	Plleasure	Pllaesure
2.	Pledje	Pledge	Plledje	Plledge
3.	Planty	Pllenty	Pllanty	Plenty
4.	Plos	Plus	Pllos	Pllus
5.	Poett	Puet	Poet	Puett
6.	Poison	Piosson	Pioson	Poisson
7.	Pollite	Polite	Pullite	Pulite
8.	Polutoin	Polution	Pollutoin	Pollution
9.	Popullatoin	Population	Populatoin	Popullation
10.	Porch	Purrch	Porrch	Purch
11.	Porridge	Poridge	Poridje	Porridje
12.	Purrtal	Portal	Purtal	Porrtal
13.	Possitive	Pousitive	Poussitive	Positive
14.	Posstal	Postal	Pousstal	Poustal

Write four sentences using as many words from your spelling list as you can. Underline the spelling words.

1. ....

2. ....

3. ....

4. ....

With permission Use an old magazine, newspaper or junk mail and find as many of your words in this unit you can (or the letters that make up your word). Cut it out, use a glue stick and paste it on your paper here.

Spelling Test

Your Answers		Correct Spelling If Incorrect	
1		1	
2		2	
3		3	
4		4	
5		5	
6		6	
7		7	
8		8	
9		9	
10		10	
11		11	
12		12	
13		13	
14		14	
15		15	
16		16	
17		17	
18		18	
19		19	
20		20	

Unit 33 Unscramble

Let's put your puzzle solving skills to the test. Try unscrambling the words using the words in the box.

Preacher	Probably	Presentation	Private	Pressure	Prey
President	Prevention	Prince	Prairie	Principle	Predator
Prime					

1. RIEIPRA   P _ _ _ r _ _

2. APCHRERE   P _ _ _ c _ _ _

3. PREADTOR   P r _ _ _ _ _ _

4. STRIENPTAEON   _ r _ _ _ _ t _ _ _ _ n

5. EPDEITSNR   P _ _ _ _ _ _ n _

6. REUSSPRE   _ _ e _ s _ _ _

7. EPNRTIEOVN   _ _ e _ e _ t _ _ _

8. EYPR   _ r _ _

9. IPERM   _ _ _ _ e

10. NRPICE   _ _ i _ _ e

11. NPRLCEPII   _ _ _ n _ i _ _ _

12. RTPEAIV   _ r _ _ _ t _

13. YOBPABRL   _ _ _ _ _ _ l y

Write a definition for each word. Underline the spelling words.

Unit 33 Wordsearch

Search the words from the given list below. Words can be across, down, diagonally and spread out.

T	N	E	D	I	S	E	R	P	F	S	V
B	L	A	T	J	M	P	D	R	I	S	R
L	E	P	R	I	N	C	I	P	L	E	R
P	F	I	R	Z	U	H	Y	E	J	P	O
R	R	P	W	R	U	Z	C	T	R	Z	T
E	P	R	E	V	E	N	T	I	O	N	A
A	V	A	S	A	I	L	V	O	D	X	D
C	Y	I	N	R	A	A	B	P	Q	Y	E
H	D	R	P	K	T	M	G	Q	G	V	R
E	X	I	S	E	R	U	S	S	E	R	P
R	Y	E	R	P	R	O	B	A	B	L	Y
N	O	I	T	A	T	N	E	S	E	R	P

Prairie	Preacher	Predator	Presentation	President
Pressure	Prevention	Prey	Prime	Prince
Principle	Private	Probably		

Unit 33 Spelling

Circle the correct spelling for each word.

	A	**B**	**C**	**D**
1.	Prrairei	Prairei	Prairie	Prrairie
2.	Prreacher	Preacher	Prraecher	Praecher
3.	Prredator	Predatur	Prredatur	Predator
4.	Prresentation	Presentation	Presentatoin	Prresentatoin
5.	Presadent	Prresident	Prresadent	President
6.	Presore	Pressure	Prescure	Presure
7.	Preventoin	Prreventoin	Prrevention	Prevention
8.	Paay	Prrey	Prey	Prray
9.	Prime	Prame	Prrime	Prrame
10.	Prrinse	Prince	Prrince	Prinse
11.	Principle	Prranciple	Pranciple	Prrinciple
12.	Private	Pravate	Prravate	Prrivate
13.	Prubably	Prrubably	Probably	Prrobably

Write four sentences using as many words from your spelling list as you can. Underline the spelling words.

1. ....

2. ....

3. ....

4. ....

With permission Use an old magazine, newspaper or junk mail and find as many of your words in this unit you can (or the letters that make up your word). Cut it out, use a glue stick and paste it on your paper here.

Spelling Test

Your Answers	Correct Spelling If Incorrect
1	1
2	2
3	3
4	4
5	5
6	6
7	7
8	8
9	9
10	10
11	11
12	12
13	13
14	14
15	15
16	16
17	17
18	18
19	19
20	20

Unit 34 Unscramble

Let's put your puzzle solving skills to the test. Try unscrambling the words using the words in the box.

Proverb	Proposal	Promotion	Protection	Public	Pumpkin
Pueblo	Program	Publish	Profession	Puncture	Produce
Puppet	Pupil				

1. DOURPEC   _ _ o _ _ _ e

2. RSPSOONFEI   _ _ o _ _ _ s i _ _

3. RAGPRMO   _ _ _ g _ a _

4. RTOPINMOO   _ r _ _ _ _ _ _ n

5. RPLAOPSO   _ _ _ _ _ s a _

6. PINROOTCET   P _ _ t _ _ _ i _ _

7. RRPBVOE   _ _ _ v _ _ b

8. PLICBU   _ _ _ l _ c

9. SUIBPHL   _ _ _ _ i _ h

10. EOLPUB   _ u _ _ _ o

11. MNUPIKP   P u _ _ _ _ _

12. TURNUCEP   P _ _ _ t _ _ _

13. PLUIP   _ u _ _ _

14. EUTPPP   _ _ _ p e _

Write a definition for each word. Underline the spelling words.

_____

_____

_____

_____

_____

Unit 34 Wordsearch

Search the words from the given list below. Words can be across, down, diagonally and spread out.

```
Y  J  I  P  L  P  R  O  G  R  A  M
V  Q  N  O  I  T  O  M  O  R  P  B
V  O  U  N  Z  N  I  K  P  M  U  P
B  R  E  V  O  R  P  P  T  A  B  I
Y  B  X  D  L  H  N  E  U  U  L  Y
B  X  Q  H  B  L  P  I  J  V  I  A
E  P  S  U  E  P  R  O  D  U  C  E
G  L  U  P  U  N  C  T  U  R  E  K
W  K  X  P  P  R  O  P  O  S  A  L
R  V  N  O  I  S  S  E  F  O  R  P
J  U  P  U  B  L  I  S  H  M  V  D
P  R  O  T  E  C  T  I  O  N  U  Z
```

Produce	Profession	Program	Promotion	Proposal
Protection	Proverb	Public	Publish	Pueblo
Pumpkin	Puncture	Pupil	Puppet	

Unit 34 Spelling

Name: _____

Date: _____

Circle the correct spelling for each word.

	A	B	C	D
1.	Produse	Prroduce	Produce	Prroduse
2.	Profession	Professoin	Profesion	Profesoin
3.	Program	Prrogram	Prugram	Prrugram
4.	Promotion	Prromotoin	Promotoin	Prromotion
5.	Prroposal	Proposal	Prropousal	Propousal
6.	Protectoin	Prrotection	Prrotectoin	Protection
7.	Pruverb	Proverb	Prruverb	Prroverb
8.	Pobllic	Poblic	Publlic	Public
9.	Poblish	Publlish	Publish	Pobllish
10.	Poeblo	Puebllo	Pueblo	Poebllo
11.	Pumpkn	Pumpckin	Pumpkin	Pumpckn
12.	Punctture	Poncture	Puncture	Ponctture
13.	Popill	Pupill	Popil	Pupil
14.	Poppen	Puppet	Popet	Pupet

Write four sentences using as many words from your spelling list as you can. Underline the spelling words.

1. ....

2. ....

3. ....

4. ....

With permission Use an old magazine, newspaper or junk mail and find as many of your words in this unit you can (or the letters that make up your word). Cut it out, use a glue stick and paste it on your paper here.

Spelling Test

Your Answers	Correct Spelling If Incorrect
1	1
2	2
3	3
4	4
5	5
6	6
7	7
8	8
9	9
10	10
11	11
12	12
13	13
14	14
15	15
16	16
17	17
18	18
19	19
20	20

Name: _____

Date: _____

Unit 35 Unscramble

Let's put your puzzle solving skills to the test. Try unscrambling the words using the words in the box.

Purple	Raccoon	Reaction	Ray	Puzzle	Quiz
Quite	Rabbit	Ration	Range	Railroad	Queen
Rainforest	Purpose	Rather	Quantity	Rancher	

1. PRULEP   P u _ _ _ _

2. EURPOPS   P _ _ _ _ _ e

3. UZPLEZ   _ _ z _ l _

4. TIUAQYNT   _ _ _ _ _ i t _

5. EENQU   _ _ e _ _

6. UEITQ   _ u _ _ _

7. QZIU   Q _ _ _

8. BBRTAI   _ _ b _ i _

9. OCONCRA   _ _ c c _ _ _

10. ORIRADLA   R _ _ l _ _ _ _

11. IOTNFRERAS   _ a _ n _ _ _ _ _ t

12. ERNARCH   _ _ _ _ h e _

13. EARNG   _ _ _ g _

14. ARRHTE   R _ _ _ e _

15. ANIROT   R _ _ _ _ n

16. ARY   _ a _

17. RANTIOEC   R _ _ c _ _ _ _

Write a definition for each word. Underline the spelling words.

_____

_____

_____

_____

Unit 35 Wordsearch

Search the words from the given list below. Words can be across, down, diagonally and spread out.

Y	V	R	A	I	N	F	O	R	E	S	T
T	G	C	R	L	M	H	P	M	C	Z	N
I	R	B	A	U	Q	U	I	T	E	E	Q
T	A	T	C	I	R	A	N	G	E	F	F
N	N	D	C	P	A	O	R	U	M	B	F
A	C	B	O	X	B	K	Q	N	D	S	Y
U	H	S	O	J	B	P	U	R	P	L	E
Q	E	V	N	X	I	X	I	E	J	M	J
E	R	W	J	L	T	W	Z	H	G	A	G
P	U	Z	Z	L	E	R	A	T	I	O	N
N	O	I	T	C	A	E	R	A	Y	I	I
Y	D	A	O	R	L	I	A	R	F	Q	S

Purple	Purpose	Puzzle	Quantity	Queen
Quite	Quiz	Rabbit	Raccoon	Railroad
Rainforest	Rancher	Range	Rather	Ration
Ray	Reaction			

Unit 35 Spelling

Circle the correct spelling for each word.

	A	B	C	D
1.	Porple	Porrple	Purple	Purrple
2.	Purpose	Purpouse	Purrpouse	Purrpose
3.	Pozle	Puzle	Puzzle	Pozzle
4.	Qaunttity	Quanttity	Quantity	Qauntity
5.	Quen	Qoen	Queen	Qiean
6.	Qoite	Quitte	Quite	Qoitte
7.	Qoiz	Quiz	Qoz	Quz
8.	Rabbat	Rabbit	Rabit	Ratat
9.	Racojn	Racoun	Raccoon	Raccoun
10.	Riallroad	Rialroad	Railroad	Raillroad
11.	Rianforest	Rianfforest	Rainforest	Rainfforest
12.	Rincherr	Rancherr	Rincher	Rancher
13.	Ranje	Rane	Riye	Range
14.	Ratther	Ritther	Rather	Rither
15.	Ration	Rattoin	Ratoin	Rattion
16.	Reacttoin	Reacttion	Reactoin	Reaction

Write four sentences using as many words from your spelling list as you can. Underline the spelling words.

1. ....

2. ....

3. ....

4. ....

With permission Use an old magazine, newspaper or junk mail and find as many of your words in this unit you can (or the letters that make up your word). Cut it out, use a glue stick and paste it on your paper here.

Spelling Test

Your Answers

1
2
3
4
5
6
7
8
9
10
11
12
13
14
15
16
17
18
19
20

Correct Spelling If Incorrect

1
2
3
4
5
6
7
8
9
10
11
12
13
14
15
16
17
18
19
20

Unit 36 Unscramble

Let's put your puzzle solving skills to the test. Try unscrambling the words using the words in the box.

Region	Really	Remember	Receive	Recycle	Reproduce
Release	Reason	Relief	Reject	Relax	Remove
Represent	Ready	Reflection	Remote		

1. YEDAR   _ _ a _ _

2. RYLLEA   R _ a _ _ _

3. AORSEN   R _ a _ _ _

4. CEIEREV   _ _ c _ i _ _

5. YRCEELC   R _ c _ _ _ _

6. ENCLOFREIT   _ _ f _ e c _ _ _ _

7. IOGNRE   _ e _ _ _ n

8. EJECRT   _ _ _ e _ t

9. RALXE   _ e _ _ _

10. AELSERE   R _ _ _ _ s _

11. LIEREF   _ e _ i _ _

12. REEMMBER   _ _ m e _ _ _ _

13. EERTMO   _ e _ o _ _

14. MREEOV   _ e _ _ v _

15. RNTPEEERS   _ _ _ _ e _ n _

16. OUPCEERRD   _ _ _ _ o d _ _ _

Write a definition for each word. Underline the spelling words.

Unit 36 Wordsearch

Name: _____

Date: _____

Search the words from the given list below. Words can be across, down, diagonally and spread out.

X	J	G	E	H	E	J	Y	C	L	R	L
P	A	O	V	X	P	S	Y	Q	E	T	E
X	R	L	I	F	I	W	A	A	P	Q	C
R	E	R	E	C	Y	C	L	E	Y	I	U
E	F	E	C	R	K	L	Y	T	L	F	D
M	L	J	E	C	Y	D	V	O	P	E	O
E	E	E	R	D	A	I	N	M	K	I	R
M	C	C	I	E	V	O	M	E	R	L	P
B	T	T	R	O	I	V	O	R	X	E	E
E	I	H	X	G	C	Q	Q	U	W	R	R
R	O	R	E	A	S	O	N	Y	G	Z	D
D	N	R	E	P	R	E	S	E	N	T	S

Ready	Really	Reason	Receive	Recycle
Reflection	Region	Reject	Relax	Release
Relief	Remember	Remote	Remove	Represent
Reproduce				

Unit 36 Spelling

Circle the correct spelling for each word.

	A	B	C	D
1.	Ready	Riedy	Raedy	Reidy
2.	Realy	Really	Raelly	Raely
3.	Raeson	Raesson	Reason	Reasson
4.	Recieve	Reseive	Resieve	Receive
5.	Recycle	Recyclle	Racyclle	Racycle
6.	Refflection	Refflectoin	Reflection	Reflectoin
7.	Region	Regiun	Regio	Regoin
8.	Reject	Regect	Rejectt	Regectt
9.	Relix	Relax	Rellix	Rellax
10.	Release	Rellaese	Relaese	Rellease
11.	Relief	Rellief	Releif	Relleif
12.	Ramember	Ramemberr	Rememberr	Remember
13.	Remotte	Remote	Remutte	Remute
14.	Remove	Remoe	Remuve	Remue
15.	Reprecent	Reprrecent	Represent	Reprresent
16.	Reprroduce	Reprroduse	Reproduce	Reproduse

Write four sentences using as many words from your spelling list as you can. Underline the spelling words.

1. ....

2. ....

3. ....

4. ....

With permission Use an old magazine, newspaper or junk mail and find as many of your words in this unit you can (or the letters that make up your word). Cut it out, use a glue stick and paste it on your paper here.

Spelling Test

Your Answers		Correct Spelling If Incorrect	
1		1	
2		2	
3		3	
4		4	
5		5	
6		6	
7		7	
8		8	
9		9	
10		10	
11		11	
12		12	
13		13	
14		14	
15		15	
16		16	
17		17	
18		18	
19		19	
20		20	

BONUS Unit Unscramble

Let's put your puzzle solving skills to the test. Try unscrambling the words using the words in the box.

Responsibility	Return	Revise	Rhombus	Robot	Ribbon
Request	Result	Resist	Rodeo	Revision	Richer
Reptile	Retain	Ridge	Robin		

1. PETEILR   _ _ _ t _ l _

2. ETEURSQ   R e _ _ _ _ _

3. SIERST   _ _ _ i _ t

4. SORETBPISINILY   _ _ _ p o _ _ i _ _ _ _ _ y

5. SLRTEU   _ e s _ _ _

6. ARETIN   _ e _ _ _ n

7. RNRUTE   _ _ _ _ r n

8. IEVESR   _ e _ _ _ e

9. IEOVNRSI   _ _ v i _ _ _ _

10. ROHBMSU   _ _ _ _ _ u s

11. BINRBO   R _ _ _ _ n

12. RECIRH   _ i _ _ e _

13. EDIRG   R _ _ _ _

14. ONIRB   _ _ b _ _

15. TOROB   _ _ _ _ t

16. DROOE   _ _ _ _ o

BONUS Wordsearch

Name: _____

Date: _____

```
E  N  R  X  S  E  Q  U  E  N  C  E
Y  S  R  O  T  A  T  I  O  N  Z  T
U  S  E  V  E  N  T  Y  W  N  K  T
Q  S  T  N  S  E  R  I  E  S  N  R
S  E  C  T  T  D  S  E  N  E  G  U
B  C  L  V  E  E  T  A  M  T  S  P
G  T  A  L  T  N  N  I  D  U  C  T
R  I  L  R  E  P  D  C  Q  D  A  U
K  O  G  V  L  E  R  B  E  H  L  R
R  N  E  M  S  E  I  Z  U  R  E  E
G  S  C  I  E  N  T  I  S  T  G  N
G  P  X  S  C  U  L  P  T  U  R  E
```

Rolled	Rotation	Rupture	Saddle	Satin
Scale	Scarlet	Scientist	Sculpture	Section
Sediment	Seizure	Sentence	Sequence	Series
Seventeen	Seventy			

BONUS Unit Spelling

Name: _____

Date: _____

Write the correct spelling for each word on the line.

	A	B	C	D
1. _____	Rolled	Roled	Rulled	Rulid
2. _____	Rotatoin	Rottation	Rotation	Rottatoin
3. _____	Rupture	Roptture	Ropture	Ruptture
4. _____	Saddle	Siddle	Sadle	Sbdle
5. _____	Sattin	Sattan	Satin	Satan
6. _____	Scale	Scalle	Scile	Scille
7. _____	Scirrlet	Scarlet	Scirlet	Scarrlet
8. _____	Scientist	Sceinttist	Sceintist	Scienttist
9. _____	Scollpture	Scolpture	Sculpture	Scullpture
10. _____	Secttion	Section	Sectoin	Secttoin
11. _____	Sediment	Sedinment	Sedimentt	Sedinmentt
12. _____	Seizure	Siezure	Siezurre	Seizurre
13. _____	Senttance	Sentance	Sentence	Senttence
14. _____	Sequence	Sequance	Seqoene	Sequene
15. _____	Series	Serriks	Serreis	Sereis
16. _____	Seventean	Seventeen	Saventen	Seventen
17. _____	Saventy	Seventty	Seventy	Saventty

BONUS Wordsearch

Name: _____

Date: _____

```
Z  S  H  O  W  N  L  S  I  X  T  Y
U  S  N  U  G  G  L  E  P  V  S  P
S  O  X  S  K  E  T  C  H  E  P  D
I  C  U  A  S  I  S  L  I  D  E  Y
G  C  S  S  S  P  E  C  I  A  L  D
N  E  S  H  E  R  I  F  F  W  L  T
A  R  I  I  O  V  E  N  O  N  I  K
T  S  N  M  X  V  E  L  A  L  N  S
U  K  C  O  L  T  S  R  P  C  G  O
R  I  E  O  D  T  E  S  A  R  H  L
E  L  S  I  M  I  L  E  Q  L  R  O
Y  L  S  H  O  R  T  E  N  P  A  O
```

Several	Sheriff	Shorten	Shown	Signature
Simile	Since	Site	Sixteen	Sixty
Sketch	Skill	Slide	Slowly	Snuggle
Soccer	Solo	Solve	Special	Speed
Spelling	Spinach	Split		

Name: _____

BONUS Unit Spelling

Date: _____

Write the correct spelling for each word on the line.

	A	B	C	D
1. _____	Severril	Severil	Several	Severral
2. _____	Sheris	Sheriphf	Sheriph	Sheriff
3. _____	Shurten	Shorrten	Shurrten	Shorten
4. _____	Shon	Sfan	Shuwn	Shown
5. _____	Signatture	Signatore	Signattore	Signature
6. _____	Simile	Samille	Simille	Samile
7. _____	Saze	Sinse	Since	Shne
8. _____	Satte	Sitte	Site	Sdte
9. _____	Sixteen	Sixtean	Saxten	Sixten
10. _____	Saxty	Saxtty	Sixty	Sixtty
11. _____	Sketch	Scketch	Skettch	Sckettch
12. _____	Skil	Sckil	Sckill	Skill
13. _____	Sllide	Slide	Sllade	Szade
14. _____	Sllowly	Slowly	Slluwly	Sluwly
15. _____	Snoggle	Snuggle	Snugle	Snogle
16. _____	Soccer	Soser	Socer	Socser
17. _____	Sulo	Solo	Sollo	Sullo
18. _____	Solve	Sollve	Sulve	Sullve
19. _____	Specaill	Specail	Speciall	Special
20. _____	Spad	Spead	Speg	Speed
21. _____	Speling	Spellang	Spelling	Spelang
22. _____	Spanah	Spinach	Spinah	Spanach

BONUS Wordsearch

```
U  Z  X  S  G  I  J  Q  S  U  R  F  A  C  E  Q
V  E  S  Z  Q  W  A  T  B  E  A  S  H  T  U  I
J  Q  H  Y  S  U  T  Q  L  X  S  U  N  U  D  S
K  M  K  F  S  S  A  K  E  A  T  B  M  M  S  W
J  Q  A  A  M  T  N  S  L  X  O  J  I  G  S  I
A  S  U  C  L  I  E  D  H  J  C  E  C  Q  B  N
N  T  H  F  R  Y  N  M  V  P  K  C  G  R  Q  G
M  R  S  P  A  S  T  O  L  E  N  T  W  Y  V  S
P  O  S  W  S  E  L  S  T  R  E  T  C  H  E  R
T  L  S  Y  E  S  U  G  G  E  S  T  I  O  N  W
A  L  T  T  K  E  S  T  R  A  W  B  E  R  R  Y
R  E  R  A  X  E  T  N  S  T  A  M  P  E  D  E
I  R  I  R  A  S  Y  M  M  E  T  R  Y  V  G  B
F  Z  K  D  L  M  D  F  N  S  Y  N  O  N  Y  M
F  U  E  Y  Z  S  K  S  T  R  U  C  T  U  R  E
P  J  S  T  E  N  C  I  L  S  T  O  R  A  G  E
```

Sprinkle	Squash	Stampede	Stencil	Stock
Stolen	Storage	Strawberry	Stretcher	Strike
Stroller	Structure	Subject	Suggestion	Surface
Sweet	Swings	Symmetry	Synonym	System
Tardy	Tariff			

Grocery Spelling List

Check the ones you can spell.
Mark X for the ones you miss.

Bread/Grains
- ☐ bread
- ☐ bagels
- ☐ pasta
- ☐ tortillas
- ☐ buns

Breakfast
- ☐ cereal
- ☐ oatmeal
- ☐ baking mix

Meat
- ☐ bacon
- ☐ chicken
- ☐ fish
- ☐ ground beef
- ☐ hot dogs
- ☐ sausage

Drinks
- ☐ coffee
- ☐ tea
- ☐ juice
- ☐ milk
- ☐ water

Dairy
- ☐ butter
- ☐ cheese
- ☐ eggs
- ☐ sour cream
- ☐ yogurt

Snacks
- ☐ chips
- ☐ cookies
- ☐ candy
- ☐ nuts/seeds

Frozen
- ☐ meat
- ☐ pizza
- ☐ TV dinners
- ☐ ice cream
- ☐ waffles
- ☐ vegetables

Cans/Jars
- ☐ fruit/vegetables
- ☐ jam/jelly
- ☐ peanut butter
- ☐ soup
- ☐ chili

Condiments
- ☐ catsup
- ☐ mayonnaise
- ☐ mustard
- ☐ oil
- ☐ salad dressing
- ☐ spices

Fruits/Veggies
- ☐ apples
- ☐ avocado
- ☐ bananas
- ☐ berries
- ☐ beans
- ☐ broccoli
- ☐ cauliflower
- ☐ celery
- ☐ cucumber
- ☐ garlic
- ☐ grapefruit
- ☐ grapes
- ☐ kiwi
- ☐ lettuce
- ☐ mushrooms
- ☐ onions
- ☐ oranges
- ☐ peaches
- ☐ peas
- ☐ spinach
- ☐ sprouts
- ☐ squash
- ☐ tomato

Misc Food Words
- ☐ _____
- ☐ _____
- ☐ _____
- ☐ _____
- ☐ _____
- ☐ _____
- ☐ _____
- ☐ _____

Check the ones you can spell.
Mark X for the ones you miss.

Bread/Grains
- ☐ bread
- ☐ bagels
- ☐ pasta
- ☐ tortillas
- ☐ buns

Breakfast
- ☐ cereal
- ☐ oatmeal
- ☐ baking mix

Meat
- ☐ bacon
- ☐ chicken
- ☐ fish
- ☐ ground beef
- ☐ hot dogs
- ☐ sausage

Drinks
- ☐ coffee
- ☐ tea
- ☐ juice
- ☐ milk
- ☐ water

Dairy
- ☐ butter
- ☐ cheese
- ☐ eggs
- ☐ sour cream
- ☐ yogurt

Snacks
- ☐ chips
- ☐ cookies
- ☐ candy
- ☐ nuts/seeds

Frozen
- ☐ meat
- ☐ pizza
- ☐ TV dinners
- ☐ ice cream
- ☐ waffles
- ☐ vegetables

Cans/Jars
- ☐ fruit/vegetables
- ☐ jam/jelly
- ☐ peanut butter
- ☐ soup
- ☐ chili

Condiments
- ☐ catsup
- ☐ mayonnaise
- ☐ mustard
- ☐ oil
- ☐ salad dressing
- ☐ spices

Fruits/Veggies
- ☐ apples
- ☐ avocado
- ☐ bananas
- ☐ berries
- ☐ beans
- ☐ broccoli
- ☐ cauliflower
- ☐ celery
- ☐ cucumber
- ☐ garlic
- ☐ grapefruit
- ☐ grapes
- ☐ kiwi
- ☐ lettuce
- ☐ mushrooms
- ☐ onions
- ☐ oranges
- ☐ peaches
- ☐ peas
- ☐ spinach
- ☐ sprouts
- ☐ squash
- ☐ tomato

Misc Food Words
- ☐ _____
- ☐ _____
- ☐ _____
- ☐ _____
- ☐ _____
- ☐ _____
- ☐ _____
- ☐ _____

Spelling Pretest

Your Answers		Correct Spelling If Incorrect	
1		1	
2		2	
3		3	
4		4	
5		5	
6		6	
7		7	
8		8	
9		9	
10		10	
11		11	
12		12	
13		13	
14		14	
15		15	
16		16	
17		17	
18		18	
19		19	
20		20	

Spelling Pretest

Your Answers

1

2

3

4

5

6

7

8

9

10

11

12

13

14

15

16

17

18

19

20

Correct Spelling If Incorrect

1

2

3

4

5

6

7

8

9

10

11

12

13

14

15

16

17

18

19

20

Spelling Pretest

Your Answers		**Correct Spelling If Incorrect**
1		1
2		2
3		3
4		4
5		5
6		6
7		7
8		8
9		9
10		10
11		11
12		12
13		13
14		14
15		15
16		16
17		17
18		18
19		19
20		20

Spelling Pretest

Your Answers

1
2
3
4
5
6
7
8
9
10
11
12
13
14
15
16
17
18
19
20

Correct Spelling If Incorrect

1
2
3
4
5
6
7
8
9
10
11
12
13
14
15
16
17
18
19
20

Spelling Pretest

	Your Answers		Correct Spelling If Incorrect
1		1	
2		2	
3		3	
4		4	
5		5	
6		6	
7		7	
8		8	
9		9	
10		10	
11		11	
12		12	
13		13	
14		14	
15		15	
16		16	
17		17	
18		18	
19		19	
20		20	

Spelling Pretest

Your Answers		Correct Spelling If Incorrect
1		1
2		2
3		3
4		4
5		5
6		6
7		7
8		8
9		9
10		10
11		11
12		12
13		13
14		14
15		15
16		16
17		17
18		18
19		19
20		20

Spelling Pretest

Your Answers		**Correct Spelling If Incorrect**
1		1
2		2
3		3
4		4
5		5
6		6
7		7
8		8
9		9
10		10
11		11
12		12
13		13
14		14
15		15
16		16
17		17
18		18
19		19
20		20

Spelling Pretest

Your Answers		Correct Spelling If Incorrect	
1		1	
2		2	
3		3	
4		4	
5		5	
6		6	
7		7	
8		8	
9		9	
10		10	
11		11	
12		12	
13		13	
14		14	
15		15	
16		16	
17		17	
18		18	
19		19	
20		20	

Spelling Pretest

Your Answers	**Correct Spelling If Incorrect**
1	1
2	2
3	3
4	4
5	5
6	6
7	7
8	8
9	9
10	10
11	11
12	12
13	13
14	14
15	15
16	16
17	17
18	18
19	19
20	20

Class: _____

Day	M	T	W	Th	F	M	T	W	Th	F	M	T	W	Th	F	M	T	W	Th	F
Date																				
Assignments																				
UNITS																				
1																				
2																				
3																				
4																				
5																				
6																				
7																				
8																				
9																				
10																				
11																				
12																				
13																				
14																				
15																				
16																				
17																				
18																				
19																				
20																				
21																				
22																				
23																				
24																				
25																				
26																				
27																				
28																				
29																				
30																				
31																				
32																				

Made in the USA
Monee, IL
05 October 2020